Living with Radiation

How to be a nuclear greenie

Charles Pope

 A catalogue record for this book is available from the National Library of Australia

Copyright © 2018 Charles Pope

All rights reserved worldwide.

No part of the book may be copied or changed in any format, sold, or used in a way other than what is outlined in this book, under any circumstances, without the prior written permission of the publisher.

Publisher:
Inspiring Publishers
P.O. Box 159, Calwell, ACT Australia 2905
Email: publishaspg@gmail.com
http://www.inspiringpublishers.com

National Library of Australia Cataloguing-in-Publication entry

Author: Pope, Charles.
    chas.pope1@icloud.com

Title: **Living with Radiation**/*Charles Pope.*

ISBN: 978-0-6482134-3-7 (pbk)

About the Author

Charles Pope BSc, MSc, BA is a retired metallurgist who has worked with radiation in the field of Nondestructive Testing (NDT). He established C W Pope and Associates Pty Ltd with his wife Robin in 1969 and retired in 1999. He professes no deep practical knowledge in nuclear engineering, medicine or health physics, but has conducted many radiation safety courses for technicians. In retirement, he became interested in the effects of ionising radiation in more detail and is concerned that much of the debate about radiation is influenced by uninformed self-styled experts who knew even less than he did.

He and Robin live in the Hunter Valley and have three daughters and eight grandchildren. He wants to help them to live in a safe and informed environment. While completing a BA in history after retirement he also developed an interest in Australia's fascinating nuclear history. His only other venture into publishing has been a family history published in 2006. His other interests include his family, playing jazz piano, tennis and photography.

★ ★ ★

Dedication

To Robin, who has tolerated the 12-year gestation period of this book as well as Meg, Jane and Caitlin and their families. May the world be a better place for my grandchildren.

★ ★ ★

Acknowledgments

This book has been 10 years in the making and many people have helped and encouraged me along the way. A book like this needs two types of critic. The first is the expert who can point out errors of fact, scientific credibility, grammar spelling and common sense. The second group are those who can tell me about the readability of a book intended for non-technical readers and give me some assurance that the eyes of potential readers will not glaze over with the technical content needed, while still retaining the integrity of the science.

In the first group I would like to acknowledge discussions with Professor Ian Lowe. This has also been the opportunity to reconnect with Ian since we were fellow students at the University of NSW where we were also participants in the notorious Drama Society revues of the early sixties. Although our views did not always align, I greatly respect his experience and integrity. His comments have prompted me to question a number of my previously strongly held views.

My near neighbour and fellow tennis tragic Jim Fredsell has worked in the nuclear industry in the USA and Australia and I hope I have eliminated most of the technical shortcomings in nuclear weapons and the nuclear power industry with his assistance. It was Jim who referred me to

Don Higson and Gordon McKenzie, formerly of the AAEC/ANSTO. Don was most generous with his experience and ideas in radiation effects, as was Gordon on instrumentation. I can only apologise to Gordon for oversimplifying the physics of measuring instruments but I had to put a fence around the content somewhere. Ian Hore-Lacey has also been most helpful in comments on the Nuclear Power industry. I am also grateful to Tim Bowden for tracking down the reference to shoe salesmen in the 1950s. The permission of ANSTO to include images of the HIFAR and OPAL is appreciated.

In the second group, I greatly appreciated the time taken by Ben Chard five years ago in looking at the first draft from a non-technical view point. His frank comments initiated the first of three rewrites to get the book into a language that the layman might better understand, with minimal jargon. I hope it worked. Warwick Cadenhead also assisted with making it as readable as possible. Peter Laver was also a willing and perceptive critic who encouraged me to complete the project, as did Harry Maltman, John Kell and Tony Macfarlane. I will be forever grateful to Barry Maitland for the DNA analogy in his novel 'Babel'.

Another unwitting inspiration has been Professor Wayne Reynolds at the University of Newcastle. After retiring in 1999 I completed a BA course majoring in History and was fascinated by Wayne's insights into our nuclear history – its connection with the Snowy Mountains Scheme, postwar reconstruction and our role in the British nuclear tests during the Cold War. I also acknowledge Lyn Fowler, my high school teacher in physics and chemistry who first introduced me to the science that underpins the narrative.

And finally, I pay tribute to the proof reading prowess of Sally Pope in dealing with my fractured syntax and bringing my terminology into the 21st Century, even if I did draw the line at 'sulphur'. Special thanks also to Alan Benn, John Kell, Ray Caldwell and Greg Searle who pointed out a some typos that did offend my sense of grammar when brought to my attention and justified a second edition.

While acknowledging all of those who have assisted, responsibility for any errors and contestable conclusions is all down to me.

★ ★ ★

Contents

Abbreviations xi

Foreword xiii

Chapter 1 - Atoms, Molecules and Waves 1

Chapter 2 - Units, Measurements and Protection 25

Chapter 3 - Radiation Applications 37

Chapter 4 - Weapons and Energy 44

Chapter 5 - Natural and Voluntary Radiation 69

Chapter 6 - Radiation Effects on Humans 76

Chapter 7 - Effects of Low Doses 95

Chapter 8 - Nuclear Accidents 115

Chapter 9 - Nuclear Politics in Australia 131

Chapter 10 – Epilogue 142

APPENDICES

A   Periodic Table of the Elements 148

B   Decay of Uranium 238 149

C   Large and small units 150

D	Derivation of the Sievert as a unit of dose	152
E	WHO List of Carcinogens	155
F	Energy Data	157
G	Known fatal incidents with ionising radiation since 1945	158
H	Fatal Radiation Events	160
I	Radiation Hall of Fame	161
J	Glossary of Terms	163

BIBLIOGRAPHY 170

INDEX 172

★ ★ ★
Abbreviations

We like to keep things short and using abbreviations. The following is a list of acronyms used in this book. As each acronym appears in the text it will be preceded by its full name, but after that you'll need to consult this list

AAEC	Australian Atomic Energy Commission (now ANSTO)
ABC	Australian Broadcasting Commission
ALARA	As Low As Reasonably Achievable
ALP	Australian Labor Party
ANSTO	Australian Nuclear Science and Technology Organisation
ANU	Australian National University
ARS	Acute Radiation Sickness
BEIR	Biological Effects of Ionising Radiation
CANDU	Canadian Deuterium Uranium
CT	Computed Tomography
DDREF	Dose-Dose Rate Effectiveness Factor
DNA	Deoxyribonucleic Acid
EMR	Electromagnetic Radiation
GM	Geiger Muller (Detector)

HBRA	High Background Radiation Area
HIFAR	High Flux Atomic Reactor
HVL	Half Value Layer
ICRP	International Commission for Radiological Protection
IAEA	International Atomic Energy Authority
IVP	Intravenous Pyelogram
LNT	Linear Non-Threshold
LQ	Linear Quadratic
MKU	Mary Kathleen Uranium
MOX	Mixed Oxides
MPD	Maximum Permissible Dose
NNWS	Mon Nuclear Weapons States
NPT	(Nuclear) Non-Proliferation Treaty
NWFZ	Nuclear Weapons Free Zone
NWS	Nuclear Weapons States
NSG	Nuclear Suppliers Group
OPAL	Open Pool Australian Light Water Reactor
PET	Positron Emission Tomography
PWR	Pressurised Water Reactor
SMHEA	Snowy Mountains Hydroelectric Authority
TLD	Thermoluminescent Device
TVA	Tennessee Valley Authority
UKAEA	United Kingdom Atomic Energy Authority
UKRC	United Kingdom Radiological Council
UMPNER	Uranium Mining, Processing and Nuclear Energy Review
UNSCEAR	United Nations Scientific Committee on Effects of Atomic Radiation
UNSW	University of New South Wales
UV	Ultra Violet

★ ★ ★

Foreword

> 'The trouble with the world is that the stupid are cocksure and the intelligent are full of doubt.'
>
> Bertrand Russell

The role of a communicator is to do three things:

First	Tell' em, what you're gonna tell 'em
Then	Tell 'em
And finally	Tell 'em what you told' em

This introduction addresses the first of these objectives. The third is the epilogue at the end and everything in between is the second.

For the last forty or so years, every time I have made the 30 km drive from my home near Maitland to Newcastle I have passed this sign:

> **HELP MAKE
> CITY OF
> NEWCASTLE
> A NUCLEAR
> FREE ZONE**

When I started research for this book the sign was quite prominent, but has since been swallowed by encroaching developments, feral shrubs and roadwork. This could be an indication of just how long this book has been in the making, but that's another story. There is a similar sign erected by the Cessnock Council as you approach that city from Maitland. Maitland seems less obsessed than its neighbours about being 'nuclear free'.

So, what do these signs really mean? If it is a wish to exclude nuclear weapons from our neighbourhood, their message is a no brainer. No right-minded person wants nuclear weapons but they are a reality. But it does not stop there. The nature of my occupation has meant that during my working life I frequently had a radioactive isotope or X-ray machine securely stowed in the back of my vehicle as I drove past. I also passed the Newcastle sign on my way to the many X-ray diagnoses that ultimately resolved the problems in my lower back, which in turn led to surgery and relief from more than a decade of crippling chronic lumbar pain in 1994. Another prominent local landmark on my daily drive was the Newcastle Oncology unit that was built in part by public subscription to treat cancer using high-energy radioactive isotopes and linear accelerators. Ensuring the safety of our industrial plants, diagnosing medical complaints and the treatment of cancer (which will affect 40% of the population and ultimately kill 20% of the population) all seem to be highly laudable objectives that justify ignoring this wish for a nuclear free zone.

Sitting between the destructive power of nuclear weapons and the lifesaving diagnosis and treatment of serious illnesses are other applications such as power generation whose roles are still controversial. The debate on nuclear power is a vigorous one, with both sides claiming the moral high ground.

I am a nuclear greenie and tend to put my faith in arithmetic rather than emotion or self-interest and the arithmetic is quite persuasive. In the area where I live we have two coal-fired powers stations, one of which is due for closure in the next five years. They have a combined maximum generating capacity of around 4,500 megawatts. Every year they

- Burn 10 million tonnes of coal
- Emit 25 million tonnes (12 billion cubic metres) of carbon dioxide
- Emit 100,000 tonnes of sulphur dioxide some of which returns as acid rain
- Emit 50,000 tonnes of nitrous oxide gases (NOX)
- Produce 400,000 tonnes of solid waste
- Release 11 tonnes of uncontrolled uranium, 50 tonnes of lead and 25 tonnes of thorium

The requirement for the same amount of nuclear energy would be to burn 60 tonnes of nuclear fuel, which would produce

- 60 cubic metres of high level nuclear waste, and
- Virtually zero carbon dioxide
- Zero sulphur dioxide
- Zero NOX gases

Other interesting numbers are:

- The port of Newcastle exports around 150 million tonnes of coal per year and in doing so exports around 200 tonnes of uncontrolled uranium

- If it were economically feasible to extract it, the trace of uranium in that coal would supply almost as much energy as the coal itself.

Australia has the largest uranium deposits and is the most geologically stable continent in the world. Later you will see how remote stable sites are the essential requisites for safe nuclear waste storage and we are in an excellent position to be part of the nuclear industry.

So, what is stopping us from even mentioning nuclear energy – the carbon-free elephant in the room - when there are 450 nuclear power stations operating in the world? Is it a fear of the unknown and memories of Chernobyl and Fukushima?

We have an ambitious target to produce all of our electricity from renewable sources of energy. Currently renewables account for around 17% of our energy compared to Norway (99%), USA (14%), UK (23%) and Germany (33%). Of our 17%, more than half is hydro for which there is very little upside in a dry flat continent. Just to maintain our current supply of electricity would require 13 times our current renewables capacity and our total power requirement will probably double every 20 years. Surely nuclear energy has role to play for the rest of the current century.

We have lived with a significant level of radiation in our environment and evolved to cope with it. Conventional wisdom is that our universe emerged from a single point of nothing around 14 billion years ago with a Big Bang, and we are still living with its radioactive by products.[1] We

---

[1]For a whimsical account of the Big Bang in layman's terms, see Bill Bryson, *A Short History of Nearly Everything*, (London, Doubleday: 2003), 10-14

also embrace radiation when we need a medical diagnosis or treatment, but still have a morbid fear of its effects elsewhere.

This fear is common when we do not understand something. People are funny animals. Sometimes we get better by just taking a placebo (dummy) medicine. We justify irrational purchases by all sorts of self-serving logic. Ignorance makes us prey to the Dunning-Kruger effect, which explains why the less we know about an issue, the more we are likely to hold extreme views about it. Those who are better informed are usually more open minded.[2]

I hope this book will help the reader to be better informed and open minded about what is technically referred to as 'ionising radiation'. (More about what this means later).

The chapters are arranged to provide what I think is the natural flow for a logical narrative. Chapter 1 attempts to describe and paint a picture of the invisible. It will also present an amateur's view of why particles can act as waves and why waves can act as particles. It also explains why nuclear events are different to chemical reactions with which we are more familiar such as combustion, corrosion and digestion. You might find this chapter hard work. It certainly was for me. If you find it too hard at the first read through, come back later and it might make more sense.

Ionising radiation affects us all and if we want to live with it we need measure and manage it. Chapter 2 describes how we measure what we cannot see, hear, feel, smell or touch. Chapter 3 tells us how we use radioactivity in medicine, industry and even the home. Chapter 4 delves into nuclear weapons and nuclear energy and might help to deconstruct

---

[2]For an interesting account of the Dunning-Kruger Effect, see http://www.abc.net.au/radionational/programs/scienceshow/the-dunning-kruger-effect/3102360, 15 June, 2017

the stories you may encounter in the media. In Chapter 5 we talk about natural and voluntary radiation in our daily life. Chapter 6 discusses the effects of ionising radiation in general terms and Chapter 7 takes this further to consider the controversial issue of just how much we should worry about small doses.

Chapter 8 reviews some of the unscripted high profile nuclear events of the last 50 years. You will see that these events rarely have a single cause and human error often features in the narrative. Why do we remember the nuclear accident at Fukushima (which killed nobody) and forget the toll of the tsunami that produced 15,894 deaths, 6,152 injured and 2,562 people missing across twenty prefectures? It also mentions some non-nuclear man-made disasters that remain almost forgotten.

Why does Australia remain resolutely anti-nuclear with a bipartisan passion yet owns 30 per cent of the world's uranium and has the best natural environment for managing the world's nuclear waste? Chapter 9 looks at Australia's fraught relationship with nuclear technology. Chapter 10 gives a few personal thoughts on the radiation issue and suggests that we worry too much about it. There has been a very fast climb up the nuclear learning curve in the last 75 years. Australia could possibly embrace nuclear technology after rational discussion. I fear that the current adversarial political environment may make this difficult, but we can but try.

WARNING!

There are some maths and diagrams included. These are necessary for a full understanding of the issues. Basic school maths is all you need to get the gist of the concepts.

If the maths or ideas are a bit difficult at first reading, don't get bogged down - skip them and come back later. If you want to study the reasoning behind the arguments, you may dig deeper and find assistance in the footnotes, bibliography and appendices. Going into too much detail interrupts the flow of the text and you will get a better overview by concentrating on the big picture and reading the details later. If, however, this book is to be credible it must use footnotes and appendices to point to the fundamental science that underpins it. To gloss over the basic science would be to engage in the same unsubstantiated sweeping statements and pejorative language that public figures, opponents and proponents of nuclear technology often use to suit their opinions. In some cases, there will be a shaded box containing 'interesting but not essential' information. Feel free to skim through these boxes if you are finding the going tough. You can always come back later. You bought the book – read it how you like.

Bold case is used in the text when a new or significant term appears for the first time, to emphasise a word or phrase vital to the narrative. There is glossary of nuclear jargon in Appendix J and Hall of Fame of those who have gone before in the nuclear journey in Appendix I.

And a final bonus:
www.youtube.com/user/scishow

Many of the topics we will discuss will be covered at this site in rapid - fire and sometimes irreverent but accessible YouTube clips. Just go to the site and enter your topic of interest and you will probably get useful information in a more interesting form than traditional print. If you are naturally curious you will also find this site a great time waster.

My motivation in writing this book came from a wish to know more and reach a personal conclusion about the opposing strong and sincerely held views on nuclear energy. I have eight grandchildren who will have to live in the world we leave behind. If you are able to decide either for or against based on the contents, the book will have done its job, **whatever your decision may be.**

It is worthwhile finishing this foreword with another quote from Bertrand Russell:

'To conquer fear is the beginning of wisdom.'

★ ★ ★

Chapter 1:
Atoms, Molecules and Waves

*"Myself when young did eagerly frequent
Doctor and saint and heard great argument
About it and about; but evermore
Came out through the same door as in I went*
                              Omar Khayyam

In this chapter we discuss how particles and waves are the source of nuclear radiation. This concept can seem a bit daunting, but it is well worth the effort to gain an understanding.

There is no doubt that Sir Isaac Newton (1642-1726) was one of most influential scientists of all time. We still use his discoveries and insights in mathematics, astronomy, physics (or "natural philosophy" as science was described in his time). He supported Descartes's corpuscular theory of light, which described light as very small particles (corpuscles). Newton's theory of light lasted for 100 years until superseded by the wave theory of Christiaan Huygens. Only Newton's prestige delayed the acceptance of Huygens's theory in Newton's lifetime.

In this chapter we discuss the concept of atomic particles and gamma radiation and come to the counter intuitive conclusion that sometimes waves can act like particles and particles can act like waves. If we can get our heads around this we are well on the way to seeing that both Newton and Huygens got it right courtesy of Max Planck's quantum theory, which united the two theories. This is just as well as there is also a widespread perception that as a man Newton was deeply neurotic, unsociable, proud and vindictive.[3]

BASIC MODEL OF ATOMS AND MOLECULES

Just as the world was once considered to be flat with Jerusalem at its centre, our understanding of the structure of atoms has undergone a major rethink over the last 100 years. We use a basic model of atomic structure that gets progressively more outdated with the discovery of new subatomic particles every few years. The old model/metaphor of a hydrogen atom shown in Figure 1.1 is still the one that I learnt at school 60 years ago, but it will suffice for the purposes of this book.

At the beginning of the 20th century the model of atom was the 'plum pudding' proposed by JJ Thomson of a positive sphere (the pudding) containing negatively charged particles (plums). A New Zealander, Ernest Rutherford, developed the model shown in Figure 1.1 in 1911. The model is relatively easy to visualise because it resembles the solar system. A modern physicist would no doubt scoff at its simplicity, but it helps non-physicists to picture what is going on.

At the centre of the hydrogen atom is the nucleus. This nucleus consists of one proton that is positively charged.

---

[3]https://www.quora.com/What-was-Isaac-Newton-like-as-a-person, (16 June 2017)

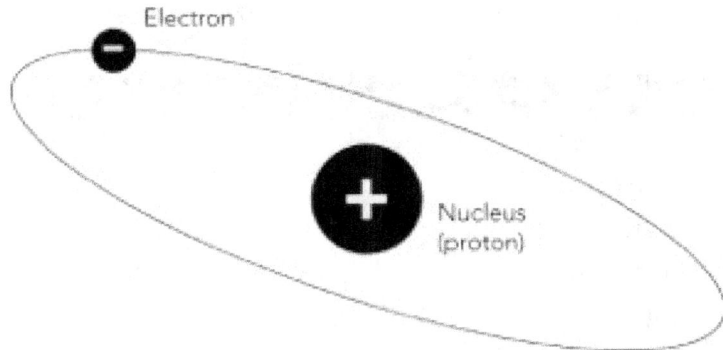

Figure 1.1: *Hydrogen atom*

Circling around the nucleus is an electron, which is negatively charged, thus balancing the positive charge of the proton, making the atom electrically neutral. To get a feeling for the scale of things, imagine a large sphere – big enough to accommodate the Melbourne Cricket Ground. At the centre of the sphere is a soccer ball representing the proton. A bee buzzing around in all that empty space would represent the electron. Any atom is about 99.9999% empty space. The full stop at the end of this sentence holds around 100 billion protons.

All **matter** is made up of a variety of atomic **elements**.[4] Each type of atom has a specific number of protons that determine its nature and properties. The number of protons of an element is called its **atomic number.** Hydrogen, Oxygen, Iron, Gold, Lead and Uranium are typical elements. There are 103 naturally occurring elements in the known universe, with more up to Ununoctium (118). These ultra-high atomic number elements do not occur naturally.

---

[4]'Matter' means the substances of which physical objects are composed – air, bones, rocks, water, plants etc. All matter is made up of atoms.

In increasing order, the first 20 elements are:

Element	Symbol	Atomic No
Hydrogen	H	1
Helium	He	2
Lithium	Li	3
Beryllium	Be	4
Boron	B	5
Carbon	C	6
Nitrogen	N	7
Oxygen	O	8
Fluorine	F	9
Neon	Ne	10
Sodium	Na	11
Magnesium	Mg	12
Aluminium	Al	13
Silicon	Si	14
Phosphorus	P	15
Sulphur	S	16
Chlorine	Cl	17
Argon	Ar	18
Potassium	K	19
Calcium	Ca	20

Note that most element symbols are obvious, but to avoid duplication some elements have less obvious names such as K for potassium and Na for sodium (from their Latin names Kalia and Natrium) as do several other elements that had been identified earlier such as silver (Ag), iron (Fe) and lead (Pb).

> **FREQUENTLY ASKED QUESTION:**
>
> **If like charges repel each other, and the nucleus is comprised of positively charged protons, why don't they repel each other. Why doesn't the nucleus fly apart?**
>
> The answer is that there are also atomic forces keeping the nucleus together (like gravity, but called 'strong nuclear forces') which are much stronger than the electrical forces that push them apart. The attraction forces are around 100 times stronger than the repulsion forces. (The things that bind the nucleus are stronger than the things that divide it to use a current political cliché.) As the number of protons approaches 100 the nucleus gets so big that the repulsive forces start to balance the nuclear forces and the nucleus becomes increasingly unstable. **It is the release of these binding forces that provides atomic energy.**

In 1869 a Russian, Dmitri Mendeleyev, recognised a pattern in this progression and developed the Periodic Table of the Elements. The pattern for the first 20 elements looked like the sequence in Figure 1.2

Orbit	1	2	3	4	5	6	7	8
1	H (1)							He (2)
2	Li (3)	Be (4)	B (5)	C (6)	N (7)	O (8)	F (9)	Ne (2)
3	Na (11)	Mg (12)	Al (13)	Si (14)	P (15)	S (16)	Cl (17)	Ar (18)
4	K (19)	Ca (20)						

Figure 1.2: *First 20 Elements of Periodic Table. The full Periodic Table is shown in Appendix A*

The full periodic table gets more complex beyond calcium but for our purposes there are two major points of interest to consider:

- Elements in the same column behave similarly in chemical reactions and are called **analogues** of each other. As an example, strontium (Sr - atomic number 38) is further down in column 2 below calcium and magnesium. Strontium can occur naturally or as a radioactive by-product of certain nuclear reactions. When discharged to the atmosphere as a fine dust it can settle on grass and be eaten by cattle, and mimic calcium. Once in the cow's digestive system it may migrate to the cow's milk and then be drunk by growing children, settle in their bones and trigger cancer.
- Elements in column 1 are metals (except for hydrogen), and are chemically highly reactive and readily react with most elements – particularly those in column 7. Typical reactions are sodium with chlorine to make sodium chloride, or sea salt and lithium with fluorine to make lithium fluoride. The product of one element combining with another is a **molecule,** also known as a compound. Other typical molecules are water (hydrogen and oxygen), carbon dioxide (carbon and oxygen) and hydrochloric acid (hydrogen and chlorine). Oxygen, nitrogen and hydrogen in the atmosphere rarely exist as single atoms, but form molecules with themselves (O_2, N_2 and H_2). Elements in column 8 are unreactive (inert) gases, which rarely combine with other elements.

Without going into the complexities, chemical reactions that form compounds occur by interaction of the orbiting

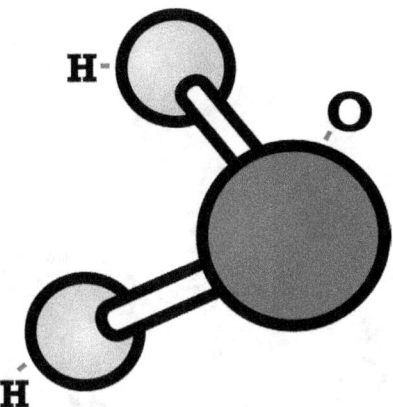

Figure 1.3: *Water Molecule*

electrons. One of the simplest molecules is water, which can be visualised in Figure 1.3. The larger oxygen atom bonds with two hydrogen atoms to produce (H_2O). Imagine two electronic hooks on the oxygen atom joining with the single hook on each of two hydrogen atoms. These are technically known as **covalent bonds** and are made by so called 'spare' electrons in the outer orbits. Just imagine the bond as joined hooks. The quality of the bond depends on the orbital electrons and any event that breaks or corrupts this electron bond threatens the integrity of the molecule. This damage process is called ionisation, and any radiation that causes such ionisation is called **ionising radiation**.

One of the most complex molecules is the **DNA** molecule, that is the basic building block of human life. As we grow, our cells keep dividing, causing our DNA to replicate from conception to death. The DNA molecule has a vast network of intersecting electron bonds and if they are corrupted by radiation, it is possible for that damage to multiply as the affected cells divide during our lifetime. This will be addressed in more detail in later chapters.

Figure 1.4: *Methane Molecule*

Figure 1.4 shows the methane (CH_4) molecule comprising one carbon atom surrounded by four hydrogen atoms. Covalent bonds are made and broken in everyday chemical processes – breathing, digestion, combustion, metal refining, corrosion, growth of human tissue, photosynthesis and many others. Methane is the principal component of natural gas. A typical reaction occurs when methane gas (CH_4), burns. The carbon-hydrogen and oxygen-oxygen bonds are broken, and new bonds are formed between carbon-oxygen and hydrogen-oxygen to produce carbon dioxide and water. The process releases a large amount of energy as heat.

$$CH_4 + 2O_2 \rightarrow CO_2 + 2H_2O + Heat$$

This promiscuous behaviour is the basis of covalent bonding in **non-nuclear** reactions. The nucleus takes no part in the reaction. As we will see later, in nuclear reactions the reaction happens in the nucleus.

ISOTOPES

The model we have looked at so far involves only protons and electrons. As an increasing number of protons determines the mass of an atom, the density (specific gravity) of the elements should be directly proportional to their atomic number – the density of lithium (3) should be exactly three times the density of hydrogen (1) and exactly half the density of carbon (6), and so on. This turned out not to be the case and baffled early researchers. The solution to this paradox was that the nucleus of an atom can contain **neutrons**, which are the same size as protons but have no charge.

Hydrogen, the simplest atom, can have either a solitary proton, one proton plus a neutron or proton plus two neutron. These variations are called **isotopes.** These were such exciting discoveries that for hydrogen the variations have specific names – deuterium and tritium – and special symbols D and T. The symbols fell out of favour as it soon became obvious that there were hundreds of isotopes scattered around the periodic table. The three isotopes of hydrogen all have the same atomic number and are equally distributed around the earth as:

Hydrogen	$1H_1$	(Mass no 1)	99.985%
Deuterium	$1H_2$	(Mass no 2)	0.015%
Tritium	$1H_3$	(mass no 3)	trace

This results in an atomic weight of 1.008 for naturally occurring hydrogen. Some published periodic tables also include the atomic weight (see appendix A).

Deuterium (H_2) and tritium (H_3) are two and three times the mass of hydrogen and when combined with oxygen they produce heavy water used in nuclear plants as a moderator and even became the subject in 'The Heroes of Telemark', a wartime thriller about the destruction of a German heavy water facility in Norway.

The important points to note about isotopes are:

- All isotopes of the same element behave identically in all chemical reactions.
- All elements occur naturally as a mixture of isotopes.
- Isotopes can only be separated by very expensive processes (enrichment).
- Most isotopes are stable.
- Some isotopes are naturally unstable.
- Some isotopes can be made unstable.

Isotopes are identified by their mass number (protons plus neutrons) with

U235	Uranium with 92 protons and 143 neutrons
U236	Uranium with 92 protons and 144 neutrons
U238	Uranium with 92 protons and 146 neutrons
Sr90	Strontium with 38 protons and 52 neutrons
Sr89	Strontium with 38 protons and 51 neutrons

The leading atomic number is unnecessary in general usage as the atomic number is defined by the element name.

RADIOACTIVITY

As mentioned earlier some isotopes are born stable, some start life as unstable and some isotopes have instability thrust open them[5]. Unstable isotopes are described as **radioactive.** Henri Becquerel, a French physicist discovered the phenomenon of radioactivity (radioactive decay) in 1896. He received a Nobel Prize in 1903 along with Marie and Pierre Curie for their work. Becquerel's mysterious radiation blackened photographic plates in the same way as light. Roentgen had discovered X-rays a year earlier and it was soon obvious that Becquerel's gamma rays were similar (but different) to Roentgen's X-rays. Roentgen named his discovery after 'X' – the unknown. Many natural and synthetic isotopes are radioactive, especially among the elements of high atomic number. While Roentgen's X-rays are all of the same type (electromagnetic radiation), Becquerel soon determined that there were three quite different forms of radiation, which he labelled alpha (α), beta (β) and gamma (γ).

Figure 1.5: *Alpha particle*

Alpha Particles (α) are the lumbering giants of radiation and are helium nuclei (He_4) emitted from the nucleus of the parent atom. They contain two protons and two neutrons as shown in Figure 1.5. Some characteristics of the alpha particle are:

---
[5]Apologies to Shakespeare.

- By sub-atomic standards it is quite large, being four times the size of a hydrogen nucleus and ten thousand times larger than an electron.
- It is ejected from the nucleus at around 15,000 km/sec, which is about one twentieth of the speed of light and quite slow by subatomic standards.
- It has a double positive charge, so is attracted to electrons, but repelled by protons in the nucleus of other atoms.
- As the alpha particle travels through matter it interacts with molecules and quickly comes to rest. This called absorption.
- Those atoms that it does interact with can be damaged by the process.
- You can stop an alpha particle with a sheet of paper due to its slow speed and large size.
- Protection from alpha particles in the open is relatively easy, but any alpha particles absorbed through eating or breathing can be damaging if they lodge in critical organs in the body.
- Polonium 210 is the alpha emitting nuclear poison of choice as it can be transported as a liquid, is safe to transport in a small glass container and will not set off conventional radiation detectors.

A real-life example of alpha decay is the spontaneous decay of naturally occurring U238:

$$_{92}U^{238} \rightarrow {}_{2}He^{4} \text{ (alpha particle)} + {}_{90}Th^{234}$$

The element symbols in this equation are preceded by their atomic number and followed by their mass number.[6]

---

[6]The leading atomic number only used for information when writing decay equations.

Uranium 238 spontaneously emits an alpha particle, and loses two protons from its nucleus, which means it is no longer uranium but has an atomic number of 90, which makes it thorium. The original nucleus has lost two neutrons as well, so the mass number is now 234, giving us thorium 234. (If in doubt, check the periodic table in Appendix A). Perhaps the old alchemists' dream of transmuting lead (atomic number 82) into gold (atomic number 79) is not so impossible after all.[7]

This decay process occurs in the nucleus whether the uranium is a pure metal, an oxide in the earth's crust, or a gas during enrichment or as a nuclear fuel. It has been occurring over the 4.5 billion years that our planet has existed and the amount of U238 remaining is about half of what it was when the earth began.

Beta Particles (β) are the mobile midgets of radiation and can be visualised as electrons emitted nucleus of the parent atom. Some characteristics of the beta particle are:

- It is small by subatomic standards, being one hundredth of one per cent of the mass of an alpha particle. It would appear as a barely visible full stop next to the alpha particle in Figure 1.5.
- It is ejected from the atom at a speed just below the speed of light and therefore has a speed 20 times the speed of an alpha particle. Imagine the electron as a rifle bullet compared to the alpha particle as a slow-moving bus.

---

[7]Turning lead into gold is not only theoretically possible. It has been achieved, but is unlikely to ever be a commercial success. See www.chemistry.about.com/cs/generalchemistry/a/aa050601a.htm (4th July 2017).

- It has a single negative charge so is repelled by other electrons, but is attracted to the nucleus.
- As the beta particle travels through matter it interacts with molecules less often than an alpha particle, but eventually comes to rest.
- The molecules with which it interacts may be damaged.
- You can stop a beta particle with a thin sheet of aluminum.
- Protection from beta particles is a little more difficult, but still relatively simple. Eating or inhaling them can be damaging if the particles lodge in a vital organ.
- Typical beta emitters are hydrogen 3 (tritium), strontium 90, strontium 89, iodine 129, thorium 234 and caesium 137.

Beta decay can be represented symbolically as:

$$_{90}Th^{234} \rightarrow {}_{91}Pa^{234} + \beta\text{-(beta particle)}$$

In this case, to preserve the atomic charge balance, one of the neutrons **acquires** a positive charge and becomes a proton. The atomic number increases from 90 to 91, which makes it protactinium. The mass number has not changed.

Attentive readers will notice that the beta decay example above is a natural consequence of the previous alpha decay of U238. The sequence of decay processes that follow the natural decay of U238 by alpha and beta particle emissions is shown in more detail in Appendix B. You can follow the whole sequence of unstable uranium 238 decaying all the way down to stable lead 206.

Gamma Rays (γ) are electromagnetic radiation (EMR).

Whereas Becquerel first thought gamma rays were particles like alpha and beta particles, they were soon identified as being more like waves. The characteristics of any gamma ray depends on its source. Some other characteristics of gamma rays are:

- They are emitted at the speed of light and have unique wavelength(s) and frequency(ies).
- The waves have no charge so are neither attracted nor repelled by protons and electrons, but they can ionise matter. The molecules with which a gamma ray interacts may be damaged.
- As the gamma ray passes through matter it interacts with other molecules and is eventually absorbed.[8]
- Depending on the source of the gamma rays, they may penetrate large thicknesses of steel – up to 10cm.
- Protection from gamma rays can be extremely important for those rays with high penetrating power.
- Typical gamma emitters are:
  o cobalt 60 – can penetrate 10cm of steel
  o iridium 192 – can penetrate 6 cm steel
- Gamma rays are produced within the human body in PET scans for medical diagnosis.
- Gamma radiation is generally viewed as an electromagnetic wave, not particle radiation. Over later years the distinction between waves and particles has become a little blurred so we will now look a little closer at electromagnetic radiation.

---

[8]This process is called Compton scattering and is the basis of radiography in medicine and industry. It also allows us to shield ourselves from radiation (see Chapter 2) – see www.ndt-ed.org/EducationResources/CommunityCollege/Radiography/Physics/comptonscattering.htm

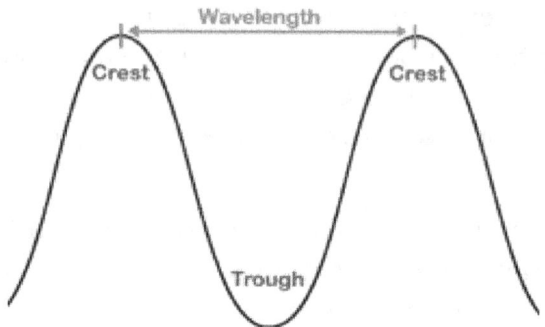

Figure 1.6: *Wave Motion*

ELECTROMAGNETIC RADIATION

To understand a little about electromagnetic radiation we also need to get a picture of something that we cannot see. We have all dropped a stone into a pond of still water and watched the ripples, or watched waves hitting the beach. This is wave motion. There is a series of ripples, each the same distance apart. If you are watching a stone in a pond, the ripples will **radiate** in circles from the stone. The stone has given up some of its energy to cause this wave pattern, and although the pond water moves up and down in much the same place, the energy radiates outwards and will cause a leaf to bob up and down. Surfers harness this same energy to catch a ride from waves that have been whipped up by winds.

There are three features of a perfectly formed wave as shown in Figure 1.6:

Wavelength (λ) is the distance between two successive crests, usually expressed in metres.

Frequency (f) is the number of times each crest passes a fixed point, expressed in cycles per second (Hertz or Hz).

Speed (c) is the rate at which this energy range is moving, measured in metres per second.

These features are connected by the equation c = f × λ

or f = c / λ
or λ = c / f

For now, just appreciate that:

The higher the frequency the shorter the wavelength and the longer the wavelength the lower the frequency.

What is of interest is that all electromagnetic radiation travels at the same speed (generally known as the speed of light) of 300,000,000 metres/second, or 300,000 km/second is a nice round number.[9] It is also a very big number. To visualise the speed of light, imagine the following:

Travelling at the speed of light,

- o you could circle the earth more than seven times in one second
- o you could get to the moon in about a second
- o you could get to the sun (147,098,290 km) in about eight minutes.

By comparison, sound is **not** EMR and travels at a fraction of this speed – typically 500 metres per second in air and 5,900 metres per second in steel.

The electromagnetic spectrum is the range of radiations from long wavelength/low frequency down to short wavelength/high frequency, or put another way, low energy to high energy. Figure 1.7 shows the range of radiations from low frequency/long wavelength AM radio at the top to ultra-high frequency/ short wavelength X-rays and gamma rays at the

---

[9] 300,000 km/second is equivalent to around ten billion km/hour.

bottom. Our area of interest in the bottom four rows (10^{-9}–10^{-12} metres). UV light that triggers skin cancers is just outside the bottom section and visible light is in a very small range between UV and infrared. The left column shows the wavelength, the second column gives an idea of the physical size of the wavelength. Other columns show the name the type of waves, source, frequency and photon energy. Forget photon energy for the moment – we'll get back to that. From now on please also ignore the other three quarters of the spectrum above – they are just there to give you the bigger picture.

Wavelength (metres)	Size	Common Name	Source	Frequency (Herz)	Photon energy (eV)
1,000(1km)				10^5	10^{-9}
100	Football field		AM Radio	10^6	10^{-8}
10	House	Radio Waves		10^7	10^{-7}
1			FM Radio	10^8	10^{-6}
0.1	Tennis Ball			10^9	10^{-5}
0.01			Oven	10^{11}	10^{-4}
0.001(1mm)	Full Stop(.)	Microwaves		10^{12}	10^{-3}
10^{-4}				10^{13}	0.01
10^{-5}	Cell	Infrared	I R camera	10^{14}	0. 1
10^{-6}	Bacteria			10^{15}	1
10^{-7}	Virus	Ultraviolet	UV Light	10^{16}	10
10^{-8}	Protein			10^{17}	100
10^{-9}		X-Rays	X-ray machines	10^{18}	1,000 (1keV)
10^{-10}	Molecule			10^{19}	10^4
10^{-11}		Hard X-rays & Gamma Rays	Linac and Gamma Rays	10^{20}	10^5
10^{-12}				10^{21}	10^6 (1MeV)

Figure 1.7: *The electromagnetic spectrum*[10]

---

[10]www.lbl.gov/MicroWorlds/ALSTool/EMSpec/EMSpec2.html (27th June 2012)

X-RAYS: MANUFACTURED EMR

We are all familiar with X-rays, and most of us will receive doses of ionising radiation at some point in our lives from the X-ray machines at the doctor or dentist's surgery and airport security. Some characteristics of X-rays:

- X-rays are traditionally regarded as wave motion like gamma rays; they have no discernible mass, they travel at the speed of light and have no electrical charge. They interact with other atoms as they pass through and can damage the atoms and molecules that they interact with. Depending on the tube voltage, X-rays can have very high penetrating power, making it important to shield ourselves from them.
- X-rays are different to gamma rays in other ways:
  o Whereas a gamma ray is determined by the source of radiation, X-rays can be generated to order within a range from soft (low-penetrating for examining the human body and thin, light metals such as aluminium) to hard (high-penetrating up to 10cm steel or for radiation therapy for cancer).
  o Gamma rays are produced at one or two specific frequencies while X-rays are produced over a range, often with a mix of soft and hard radiation.
  o X-rays are 'fail safe'. If the X-ray machine fails, radiation stops, whereas gamma rays continue without interruption. When not in use gamma sources must be contained in a shielding device.

If you are interested in how X-rays are produced, see Figure 1.8. Medical X-rays generally use lower energy (low voltage, typically 50 kV), while industrial X-rays can be up to 300 kV or as much as one megavolt by using special

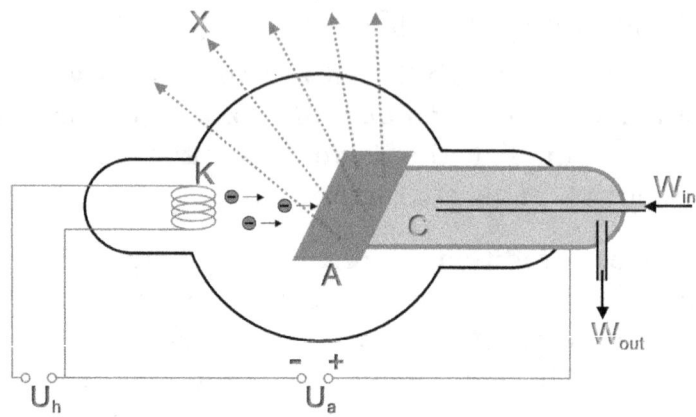

Figure 1.8: *Traditional Coolidge (X-Ray) Tube*

high voltage equipment such as linear accelerators. A glass vacuum tube encloses a negative filament (K) and positive target (A), which is mounted on a cooling element (C).

The heated filament emits electrons that are accelerated to very high velocities and they strike the target (typically tungsten mounted on a copper block). Most of the energy produced is heat, but a small proportion is converted to X-rays (X). The heat is conducted away and cooled (W_{in} and W_{out}). The accelerating voltage determines the ranges of wavelengths (energy) of the X-rays.

> MISCONCEPTIONS ABOUT EMR
>
> There is no residual radiation left in matter that has been subjected to gamma or X-rays. Think of it as light – another electromagnetic radiation. When you turn the lights off at night, things do not glow in the dark. We know a lot about the ionising effects of X- and gamma rays, but radio waves from transmission towers, mobile phones and microwaves in the kitchen have **not** been demonstrated to have deleterious effects on humans despite claims to the contrary

PARTICLES OR WAVES – SIMILAR…. BUT DIFFERENT?

> *We have no right to assume that any physical laws exist, or if they have existed up until now, that they will continue to exist in a similar manner in the future*
>
> Max Planck

Finally, we must introduce a strange concept.

At the beginning of this chapter we mentioned that Newton had been overtaken by events after he postulated his corpuscular concept of light. He saw light as made of very small particles that bounced around the universe giving illumination. Huygens lost the debate just because he disagreed with the highly-esteemed Newton. Later developments would favour Huygens – something that would have infuriated the volatile Newton, who was accustomed to intellectual superiority.[11]

> Quantum theory was the brain child of Max Planck, a German Jew who received the Nobel Prize for physics in 1918. Even more amazingly, he survived the Holocaust even though his son Erwin was executed in 1945 for his part in a failed assassination attempt on Hitler. Planck died peacefully in post war Germany. Planck's contribution (among others) was to link the energy of a **photon** of an electromagnetic wave with its frequency using Planck's constant. This number is preceded by 34 zeroes after the decimal point so it is a very small number.
>
> $$E = h \times f$$

---

[11] For a commentary on the debate see http://www.studyphysics.ca/newnotes/20/unit04_light/chp1719_light/lesson57.htm (17 June 2017)

> Where:
> E = is the photon energy
> h = is Planck's constant (0.00000000000000000000 0000000000000006626176)
> f = is the radiation frequency

So, perhaps Newton was also right – it just needed Planck to see the really big picture.

The advent of quantum theory has allowed us to apply wave properties to particles and particle properties to waves through the concept of the photon. A photon is a 'quantum' or very small quantity of energy, which makes a nonsense out of the cliché to take a 'quantum leap'. There is no need to worry about quantum theory – this is the domain of Planck and others. Without knowledge of quantum mechanics, we would not have lasers and many of the other beneficial devices of modern living. Simply accept the fact that light and other EMR can be viewed as waves or small packets of energy – a bit like a cyclist who can sometimes act like a car and sometimes like a pedestrian.

The unit of photon energy is the electron-volt (eV). Go back to the diagram of an X-ray machine in Figure 1.8. Imagine that the voltage between the filament (K) and the positively charged target (A) is one volt; the negative electron would hit the target with an energy of one electron-volt (eV). This is a very small amount of energy. If it were to be accelerated by 100 kilovolts (100,000 volts) the electron would generate a packet of energy with a photon energy of 100 keV (100,000 electron-volts). Figure 1.9 shows how the photon energy of alpha particles, beta particles, gamma rays and X-rays compare.

**The higher the photon energy,
the greater its damage potential.**

Type	Example	Typ Energy (keV)	Source/Application
α particle	Ra226	5,000	Decay product U238
β particle	Sr90	500	Nuclear fallout
γ rays X-rays	Co60 Ir192 100 kV 300 kV 1,000 kV	1,300 200 and 600 100 (max) 300 (max) 1,000 (max)	Oncology, Industrial radiography Industrial radiography Medical radiography Industrial radiography Linear accelerators

Figure 1.9: Relative photon energy of ionising radiations

Some key points on radioactivity and EMR:
- The high **photon energy** of ionising radiations allow them to penetrate human tissue and adversely affect living cells.
- The energy of a photon of visible light is a million times greater than a photon of energy from your microwave oven, and 10,000 times greater than a photon of energy from your mobile phone.
- The energy of a photon of high frequency gamma rays is a million times greater than a photon of visible light, and a billion times more than a photon of energy from your mobile phone.
- Ultraviolet radiation is a known cause of skin cancers (melanomas). Fortunately, it is relatively simple to shield ourselves from the sun's ultraviolet rays by 'slipping on a shirt, slopping on some sunscreen and slapping on a hat' in accordance with the old summer skin cancer campaign.

- There is a small technical difference between X- and gamma rays. Both are EMR, but whereas X-rays are a spectrum of photon energies generated by an electric generator using an X-ray tube, gamma rays are specific photon energies produced by the decay of natural or artificially produced radioactive materials.

Newton is no doubt having the last laugh, thanks to Planck and Einstein.

This chapter has covered the basic concepts of electromagnetic radiation (heat, radio, light, microwaves, X-rays and gamma rays), of which gamma rays and X-rays are classified as ionising radiations. If you have travelled this far unscathed, congratulations! If it has been a struggle, please do not get too disheartened – come back later after a few more chapters and it might make more sense when we get onto the more practical issues of measuring, protecting and understanding the issues in living with radiation.

★ ★ ★

Chapter 2:
Units, Measurements and Protection

If you can't measure it you can't manage it.
                                Old management myth

This may or may not be true about business, but it certainly applies to radiation technology. Many of the fears that surround the nuclear industry are due to uncertainty about what the measurements mean. Further confusion arises because the USA persists with the old original imperial units while the rest of the world has moved on to metric (SI) units, so comparing the Three Mile Island accident on one hand with Fukushima and Chernobyl on the other can be confusing. We will stick to the internationally recognised SI units, with occasional reference to the older units if necessary. Both sets of units honour the pioneers of radioactivity such as Roentgen, Curie, Becquerel, Gray and Sievert.

Radioactive decay occurs by emission of particles and/or waves in a series of discrete events called **disintegrations**. Each disintegration produces a photon of energy. Typical photon energies are shown in Figure 1.9. One disintegration per second is an activity of one becquerel (1 Bq). For any specific isotope, the activity in becquerels is a measure of the ionising energy released per second for that isotope. Decay is a random process at the atomic level but at our level of measurement it can be reliably predicted. If you could listen to the decay of a one Bq source, it would not send a signal exactly every second, like a clock ticking precise seconds. It would sound like a very erratic series of clicks, which over time averages one click per second. (You can do this in some museums). The becquerel is a very small unit, so most isotopes have activities measured in gigabecquerels (GBq) or billions of disintegrations per second. Refer to Appendix C for more details on very small and very large units. The original unit for activity was the curie (Ci). One curie is equivalent to $37 * 10^9$ (37 Gbq). The

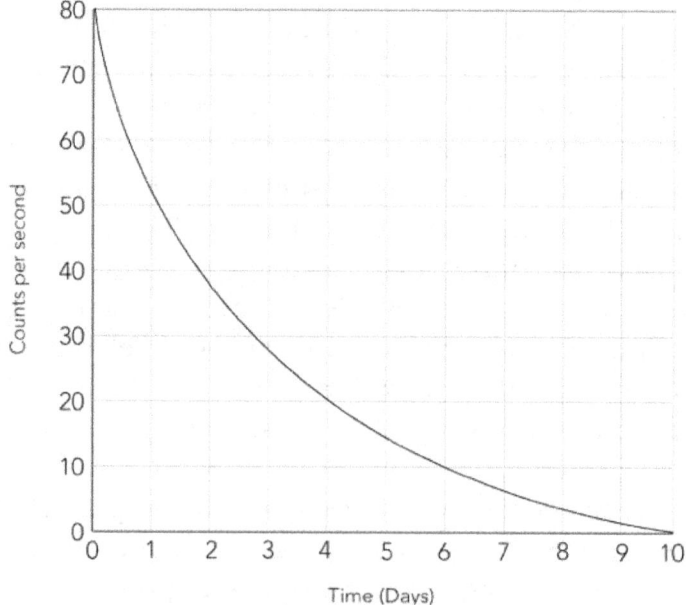

Figure 2.1: *Typical Decay Curve*

curie is still used in the USA, and while it is a pity to have lost Madame Curie's name as the unit, Becquerel is a worthy successor.

As radioactive isotopes undergo decay, the remaining activity is reduced, but never reaches zero. For that reason, we cannot specify the ultimate life of any radioactive isotope. Instead we use a measure called the **half-life** to measure the useful life of an isotope. In one half-life period, an isotope reduces to half its starting activity, in two half-lives it has reduced to one quarter, three half-lives to one eighth. Figure 2.1 shows a typical decay curve – for a hypothetical isotope of activity 80 Bq with a half-life of two days. After two days the activity is reduced to 40Bq, after four days to 20Bq etc. Extending this to 20 days (10 half-lives) it would be down to 0.08Bq - approximately one thousandth of its original activity.

There are some very important implications in the concept of half-life:

- Long half-lives are economically desirable for prolonged medical and industrial applications when there is no risk of accidental interaction with human tissue. Cobalt 60 has a half-life of 5.3 years and is used in medical oncology and industrial applications.
- Short (but not too short) half-lives are used for invasive medical procedures where rapid decay will minimise total radiation damage to the patient. Technetium-99 has a half-life of only six hours and is a radioactive tracer used for assessing blood flow. It quickly dissipates in the human body. (This also involves logistic planning to rapidly produce, deliver and administer the radioactive source at a useful activity).

- For radioactive isotopes in the environment, a short half-life means a rapidly decreasing radioactivity, and while the immediate hazard may be higher, harmful radioactivity will be of shorter duration. A long half-life means that the element may be around for many years, but could well have a relatively very low hazard, as the rate of disintegration is very low. Expressed another way, for any isotope, activity ***is inversely proportional to its half-life.***
- **Toxicity depends on dose, not half-life**. You may have a modest cellar of excellent wine, but the hazard to your health comes from how quickly you drink it, not from how many bottles are in the cellar. A cellar full of wine drunk prudently over many years (long half-life – low activity) will do much less damage to the liver than a cellar emptied in a short-term binge (short half-life – high activity).
- We have been living with radioactive materials in the earth's crust since the planet was formed.

HALF-LIVES IN NATURE:

This allows us to revisit U238 decay (Appendix B) to get a feel for the half-lives of the original U238 and its intermediate decay products. This shows some interesting features:

U238 to Th234 decay has a half-life of 4.47 billion years, which means that there has only been slightly more than one half life for this isotope since our planet was formed 4.5 billion years ago, and about 50% of the original U238 is still in the earth's crust waiting to decay.

> The next decay from Th234 to Pr234 has a half-life of 24.1 days. This means that nearly every atom of Th234 that has been painstakingly produced from U238 over the life of our planet has rapidly decayed into Pr234, and there will be very little Th234 resulting from the original U238 on the planet.
>
> The half-life of polonium 214 is a mere 163 millionths of a second (163 microseconds) and although it is a naturally occurring substance there is only a minute trace in existence at any time.

RADIATION DOSE – THE SIEVERT

Each gamma radiation has its unique photon energy (ionising potential), and one Bq of activity from Co60 gamma rays has a much higher photon energy than one Bq from Ir192. The greater the photon energy, the greater the ionising effect. The **sievert** (Sv) is the dose equivalent unit we use in practice. If you are interested, more detail about the derivation of the sievert is given in Appendix D. It takes account of the relative ionising effects of alpha, beta, gamma and X-radiation and when we talk about radiation dose (exposure equivalent) we talk in sieverts.

If using US units, the original unit for dose was the rem. One sievert is equivalent to 100 rem.

A sievert is a very large radiation dose, so we generally talk in millisievert (mSv) as our standard long term dose unit and microsievert (μSv) for very low doses. Figure 2.2 shows some typical doses in sieverts and millisieverts.

SITUATION	DOSE(mSv)	DOSE (Sv)
Fatal dose to firemen at Chernobyl (1986)	10,000 single dose	Up to 10 single dose[12]
Max dose to other workers at Fukushima	700 single dose	0.7 single dose
Six TEPCO workers at Fukishima	250 single dose	0.25 single dose
Max dose permitted by law for a radiation worker	20 mSv/yr	0.02 Sv/yr
Abdominal/lumbar CT scan	10 single dose	0.01 single dose
Residual radioactive material at Chernobyl (2000)	5 mSv/yr	0.005 Sv/yr
Barium enema	7 single dose	0.007 single dose
Typical environment background radiation	2 mSv/yr	0.002 Sv/yr
Chest X-ray	0.02 single dose	0.00002 single dose

Figure 2.2: *Typical Dose Measurements*

Protection from radiation is achieved by three basic strategies – shielding, distance and limiting the time of exposure.

Shielding is achieved by an intermediary barrier as all matter absorbs radiation. For alpha particles, clothing cover provides adequate protection as long there is neither inhalation nor swallowing of any radioactive particles. Similarly, a thin sheet of aluminium will give us protection from beta particles.

X- and gamma rays are quite a different matter, as some gamma radiations will penetrate over 10cm of steel. If we want to shield ourselves from gamma radiation, the best shielding materials are those of high mass number. Traditionally, lead (Pb) was the shielding material of choice. Depleted uranium (U238) - a residue of uranium

---
[12]This an estimate due to unavailability of measuring instruments at Chernobyl.

enrichment has been used for containment with its much higher absorption, but has its own problems as it is pyrophoric (may burst into flames when machined).

The measure of shielding capacity is the half value layer (HVL), which is the thickness of shielding material required to absorb half of the radiation. It is not possible to give accurate HVLs for X-rays as absorption depends on the design and mix of photon energies of the X-ray source, but the Ir192 values give a safe guide for industrial X-rays.

Radiation	Shielding Material	HVL (cm)
Co60 – gamma radiation	Steel	2.0
	Concrete	6.5
	Lead	1.2
Ir192 – gamma radiation	Steel	1.2
	Concrete	4.5
	Lead	0.5

Figure 2.3: *Half Value Layers for typical gamma ray sources*

Using this data, we can design enclosures to reduce exposure from radioactive materials. For example, if we want to reduce the dose rate to one thousandth (0.1%) of its level, we can use 10 half-value layers to do so. Co60 shielded with lead that requires 10 * 1.2 = 12 cm of lead. We could achieve the same result with 65 cm of concrete.

Self-absorption occurs where there is a large mass of radioactive material. If you were confronted with a large pile of material understood to be radioactive, you would intuitively think that a large pile was twice as hazardous as a pile half its size. They are probably not much different, as the outer material would absorb most of the radiation from within the pile. The only radiation reaching the outside would the radioactivity from close to the surface. The

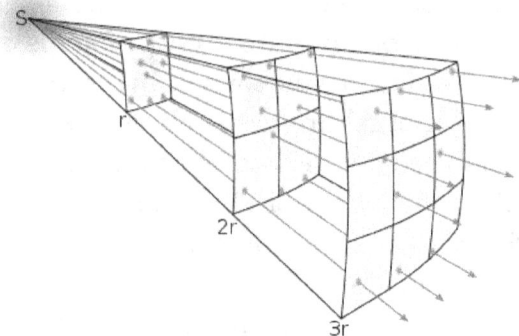

Figure 2.4: *Inverse Square Law*

other side to this coin of course is that dispersed radioactive particles such as dusts in uranium mining would be much more hazardous than the same amount of dust contained within a single pile.

Distance is another great protective strategy. A flash is useless for photographing a rock concert beyond the mosh pit as the light rapidly dissipates with distance. Similarly, ionising radiation emanating from its source is quickly dissipated. Figure 2.4 shows just how rapidly this loss in intensity occurs. Imagine a point source of radiation (S). By the time the radiation has travelled a distance 'r' it has a certain intensity. By the time it has travelled twice that distance the intensity is reduced to one quarter and at three times the intensity is reduced to one ninth. By the time it has travelled ten times the distance, the intensity will be reduced to one hundredth (1%). This is a demonstration of the power of the inverse square law.

Distance is a simple and effective way of reducing radiation dose rate. By the same logic, proximity is a powerful way of increasing the dose rate and a good reason to never touch or come too close to even very weakly radioactive materials. This is also why any radioactive material inhaled or ingested is much more toxic if it lodges near a vital organ. The dose rates tabled in Figure 2.5 show how a dose rate of 1 mSv/h, at a distance of one metre from a radioactive source, can become one million mSv (1,000 Sv) at 1 mm from its target. Similarly, the radiation source at 1 km would be one millionth of the dose rate at one metre.

Distance (metres)	Dose rate (mSv/hour)
0.001 (1 mm)	1,000,000 (10^6)
0.01 (1 cm)	10,000 (10^4)
0.1 (10cm)	100 (10^2)
1.0	1.0
10	0.01 (10^{-2})
100	0.0001 (10^{-4})
1000 (1 km)	0.0000001 (10^{-6})

Figure 2.5: *Effect of Distance on Exposure Dose*

> The inverse square law is also bad news for music fans listening through ear buds. The risk of damage with ear buds (around 8 dB) is much the same as 85 dB in the front row at a live concert.

Time is a third strategy and can be useful by limiting number of diagnostic procedures to the minimum. In the public mind there is an increasing expectation that every patient needs an X-ray or CT scan for every ache and pain, but we should avoid any unnecessary X-rays. In industrial situations people should be isolated from radiation hazards for all but essential purposes.

WHAT DOES THIS ALL MEAN?

It is no great intellectual leap from the three principles of shielding, distance and time to see three strategies for protection from ionising radiation. Storing radioactive materials behind absorbent materials (shielding), locating storage facilities away from populated areas (distance) and restricting access (time) allows very effective shielding. We will now look at measuring equipment.

MEASURING INSTRUMENTS

There are many instruments used for measuring radiation doses, all of which use the ionising properties of radiation. These can work by blackening a film, discharging a capacitor, conducting an electric current or reacting with a phosphor.[13] There are two main types of measuring device and each plays a significant role in radiation protection.

The **Geiger counter** (Geiger-Muller Tube or GM Tube – see Figure 2.6) uses the property of enabling gases to conduct electricity when ionised by radiation to form ion pairs. The negatively charged electrons are attracted to the anode and the positively charged ions move to the cathode. The tube has a central wire electrode and an encircling tubular electrode.[14] The meter is calibrated in radiation dose units (typically mSv/h) and indicates an instantaneous **dose rate** like the speedometer in a car. More modern GM devices incorporate circuitry and software to display the integrated (total) dose over time. Many GM devices incorporate audible or flashing alarms to indicate when a certain dose rate threshold has been reached. GM Tubes are the workhorses of measurement of most radiation but are less reliable for

---

[13] A phosphor is a material that exhibits luminescence, such as radar and old style TV screens.

[14] GM Tubes are a subject on their own, but for an introduction see https://en.wikipedia.org/wiki/Geiger%E2%80%93M%C3%BCller_tube July 2017.

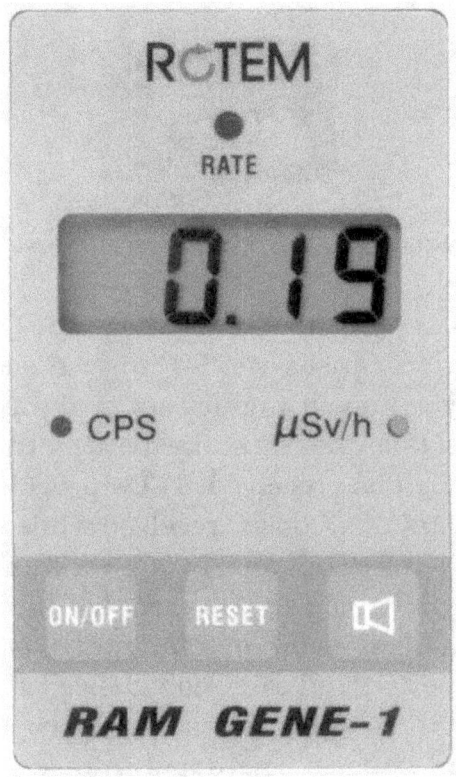

Figure 2.6: *Geiger Muller (GM) survey meter*

X-rays. Despite these limitations, GM tubes remain the preferred instrument for measuring radiation dose rates. Instruments such as the Geiger counter are referred to as 'survey meters' as they are used to measure **dose rate**. Dose rate may be measured in milliSieverts per year, hour or other time units depending on the application.

The most popular method of measuring an individual's personal radiation dose is the **thermoluminescent dosimeter** (TLD). The user wears a small badge containing a quantity of thermoluminescent material (usually lithium

Figure 2.7: *Thermoluminescent Dosimeter*

fluoride – LiF). A typical TLD is shown in Figure 2.7. Any ionising radiation causes the LiF to lose electrons, which are trapped by a known impurity. The device is processed by heating in a laboratory and measuring the light emitted to determine the dose received. TLDs provide a permanent record of the total of all doses received while wearing it and are required by law to be worn by all workers using ionising radiation. They have the advantages that they are accurate, provide a permanent record of total integrated dose received over a known period and are unobtrusive for the user. More recent TLDs can also be re-read. They replace the traditional blue film badges. The disadvantage is that they do not give an instant record of dose, but need to be processed by a third party and readings may be delayed.[15]

In summary:
- The GM tube for instant measurement of **dose rate** – like the speedometer in your car – you read as you go.
- The TLD for measurement of total **dose** received over a period – like the trip meter in your car but only readable by a third party after the trip.

---

[15]For more details on TLDs, see http://www.ndt-ed.org/Education Resources/CommunityCollege/RadiationSafety/radiation_safety_equipment/thermoluminescent.htm (15 Jun 2017)

★ ★ ★

Chapter 3:
Applications of Radiation

HOW BAD FOOD LED TO A NOBEL PRIZE:
(Do not try this at home)

'During his trying experiences at Manchester, George de Hevesy, a Hungarian physicist grew distinctly unhappy with the boarding house where he stayed. He became convinced that his landlady had a nasty habit of recycling food. One day, Hevesy secretly spiked the leftovers on his plate with radioactive material. A few days later, the electroscope he smuggled into the dining room revealed the presence of the tracer - radioactive hash! Confronted with the irrefutable evidence, all the landlady could do was exclaim 'this is magic!' The first radiotracer investigation had successfully followed leftover meat from the Sunday meal to the kitchen meat grinder, into the hash pot, and back onto the dining room table. To this day, it is doubtful if a successful radiotracer study has provided greater personal satisfaction!'[16]

---

[16]www.orau.org/ptp/articlesstories/hevesy.htm (7th June 2017) from

We will never know what happened to his landlady, but Hevesy went on to win the Nobel Prize for Chemistry in 1943 for his work on radioactive tracers. We live in a world of nuclear activity and Hevesy was a real pioneer.

Figure 3.1: *1950s shoe-fitting fluoroscope*

At a more mundane level, how many of us can remember the X-rays used to check the fit of new shoes at the big department stores in the fifties? They were all the rage at that time and I recall the one at David Jones was one of the attractions of a trip to Sydney. There was a recess for the feet at the bottom and three viewing tubes – one for the shoe fitter, one for the parent and one for the child. The child received a dose of 120 mSv/hour to the feet and lesser doses to the rest of the body.[17] The shoe fitter received a much lower dose, but received it many times a day.

'Tales from the Atomic Age'
[17]*Baring the Sole – The Rise and Fall of the Shoe – Fitting Fluoroscope,*

Do you have a smoke detector at home? It most probably uses americium 241. This isotope emits alpha particles to a sensor. If any foreign particles come between the emitter and the sensor they block the passage of alpha particles. Smoke is sufficient to absorb alpha particles and the detector sounds an alarm.

These days nuclear technology is used in much more sophisticated ways and a few will be mentioned here. There is a wealth of resources on the internet describing nuclear applications of isotopes and X-rays, and a Google search will be far more productive than extensive detail in a traditional style book.

APPLICATIONS IN MEDICINE

X-rays have been widely used for a long time, and most of us have had an X-ray at some point in our lives. Some techniques use **high-density tracers**, which are swallowed to follow the digestive system or injected into the blood stream for assessing blood circulation. Any blockages are then revealed by an X-ray, which shows where the tracer has been obstructed. The most commonly used radioisotope is technetium-99 for identifying blood blockages in musculature. Estimates are that this procedure is used 45 million times annually world-wide. Unfortunately, the half-life of technetium-99 is only six hours. This does not give time to transport and deploy the material, but does limit the dose to the patient. The ingenious solution is to supply the hospital with their own generator containing molybdenum-99 with a half-life of 66 hours. The

---

JacalynDuffin and Charles R RHayter, Isis 2000, 91:260-282. The History of Science Society.

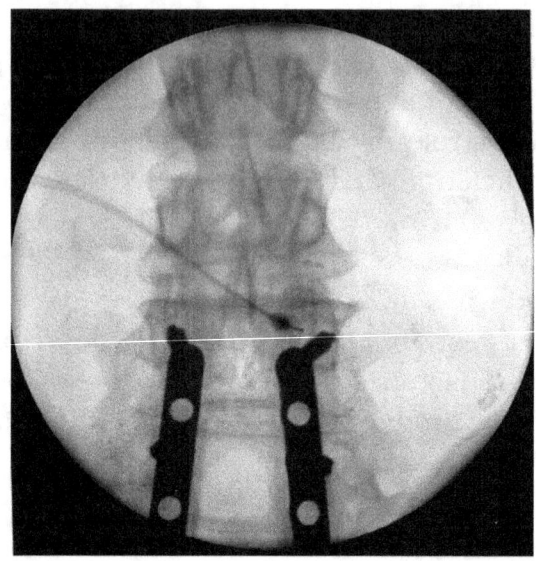

Figure 3.2: *Real time radiography during an injection*

molybdenum-99 produces technetium-99, which is harvested at the hospital and injected into the patient's blood stream.

For many years I suffered crippling back pain, for which part of the ultimate diagnosis and surgery used X-rays as well as MRI. The surgery involved screwing two metal plates into the spine. Some years after surgery I needed a cortisone injection. The doctor used real-time X-rays to guide the injection precisely through the bones and metalwork. The X-ray in Figure 3.2 shows the spinal column, two steel implants, screws and the injection point adjacent to a metal plate.

Three-dimensional X-ray images can be built up using **computed tomography** (CT) techniques in which the X-ray generator rotates around the patient and takes multiple exposures, which are then processed by computer.[18] A typical application of CT is for detecting brain traumas. The patient remains still while the X-ray source rotates around the subject area and directs the beam to a sensor, which then stores the radiation detected. Intensive computer analysis then reproduces a series of slices of the area of interest – rather like successive layers in a sliced salami.

Positron emission (PET) scans are used to examine processes within the body. This means knowing about a new particle – the positron. We won't even try to explain here what a positron is. It's described as a positively charged electron produced by decay. The patient is injected with fluorodeoxyglucose (FDG). The positrons react with electrons in the body to produce gamma rays that are detected and displayed to locate any abnormalities – particularly cancers

Oncology (treatment of cancers) is another application of ionising radiation. The patient receives a large dose (up to 50 Sv) of highly localised radiation to kill cancerous cells. External sources of radiation include very high voltage X-rays from a linear accelerator, or high-energy gamma rays with similar energy from cobalt 60. The photon energies of the two decays from Co60 are 1.17 and 1.3 MeV. Very high voltage X-Ray machines called linear accelerators are another source of radiation for oncology. Internal treatments include brachytherapy, in which an isotope is placed at the cancer site – often used in prostate or breast cancer therapy. A similar procedure

---

[18]For a guide to CT and associated procedures see https://www.insideradiology.com.au/computed-tomography/ 16 June 2017

is used by veterinary surgeons for treating cancers in animals.[19]

> ### FREQUENTLY ASKED QUESTION
> **How can relatively small doses of radiation cause cancer, when very high doses are used to *treat* cancer?**
>
> When we talk about doses in general, it generally refers to a 'whole body dose' and all the body (or at least a significant part of it) receives the same dose. Radiation therapy administers a very high dose in a very narrow beam to the precise location to destroy the cancer while not irradiating the rest of the body. A single treatment may deliver as much as 50 Sv over an area of around 5 mm square. For this reason, it is not possible to treat leukaemia with radiation therapy as the cancer is distributed in the blood stream.
>
> The patient will probably feel a degree of radiation sickness or fatigue from each treatment, but this is a case of the benefit outweighing the risk.

Another common therapy is for bone cancer that has spread (metastasised) from other cancers. An injection of **strontium 89** (Sr89) into the blood stream inserts a relatively short half-life beta particle emitter that is a chemical analogue for calcium. The strontium concentrates in the bone structure to alleviate pain in bone cancer sufferers. **Iodine 131** (I131) is a Jekyll and Hyde isotope in that it is a

---
[19]See https://www.slideshare.net/abishadh/cobalt60-external-beam-radiation-therapy June 14 2017

carcinogen causing thyroid cancer in children but also has a therapeutic role in treating the same cancer.

APPLICATIONS IN SCIENCE

Carbon 14 is of minor environmental concern, but of some scientific use to estimate the age of old organic material. Stable C12 and radioactive C14 exist in the same proportion in the bones of all living things. At death, the body manufactures no new carbon. The amount of C12 is constant but radioactive C14 decays with a half-life of 5,700 years. If the relative proportions of C12 and C14 can be measured, the age of the bone can be estimated. Because of the relatively long half-life of C14, this technique can be used to estimate organic matter up 100,000 years old – approximately 17 half-lives.

APPLICATIONS IN INDUSTRY

Radioisotopes and X-rays are also used extensively in industry to check the quality and safety of welds, castings and assemblies in power plants, pipelines, refineries, oil rigs and aircraft. Your baggage is also X-rayed for security, so all flights are made much safer by nuclear technology. The absorption properties of radioactive emissions can also be used to monitor the level of storage bins

★ ★ ★

Chapter 4:
Nuclear Weapons and Energy

Nuclear weapons are the high-profile application of nuclear technology. They grabbed the world's attention in 1945 with the atomic bombs dropped on Hiroshima and Nagasaki.[20]

Nuclear energy offers a way of low-carbon power generation, but suffers an image problem. Although this chapter mainly describes the uranium fuelled nuclear industry, there are other possible candidates for nuclear fuel and similar principles apply.

The electricity from nuclear energy is still generated by steam turbines, but the steam is generated by a nuclear reaction rather than by burning coal or gas. Uranium mining and treatment requires traditional processes to separate the uranium ores from the surrounding waste materials followed by more sophisticated enrichment to increase the concentration of U235, the active fuel ingredient. As all isotopes of uranium behave the same chemically, the enrichment process is tedious and energy intensive. The nuclear process that produces energy is called nuclear fission

---

[20]For an excellent account of the politics and events surrounding Hiroshima and Nagasaki see: Paul Ham, *Hiroshima Nagasaki*, (Sydney: Harper Collins, 2011)

(fracturing) of atoms of high atomic number. Later hydrogen (thermonuclear) weapons use nuclear fusion of low atomic number elements initiated by a nuclear fission explosion.

URANIUM THE METAL

Uranium is a metal, first discovered in 1789, and takes its name from the planet Uranus. It was derived from pitchblende, an ore associated with silver mining.[21] Uranium was first separated as a pure metal in 1841, and is one of the densest (highest specific gravity) of the naturally occurring elements. It occurs naturally as three isotopes – U234, U235 and U238, and comprises 3 parts per million of the earth's crust. The early applications of uranium were for colouring in pottery and glass making.

Uranium was first used for weapons in the atomic bombs of 1945. The first electricity from uranium was generated in 1951, with the first commercial generation in the USSR in 1954.

Mining and enrichment is called the 'front end' of the uranium cycle. One hundred years ago uranium was a waste product from the production of radium, which was much valued for its supposed therapeutic properties. Before World War II, tonnes of uranium were consigned to waste dumps to produce just one gram of radium. One such waste dump remains a source of controversy in Hunters Hill, a suburb of Sydney.[22]

The uranium cycle for nuclear power is shown in Figure 4.1. It involves mining and concentration, conversion

---

[21]Pitchblende is an oxide of Uranium – U_3O_8

[22]http://www.smh.com.au/environment/radioactive-waste-haunts-hunters-hill-residents-20111029-1mpb6.html September 2017

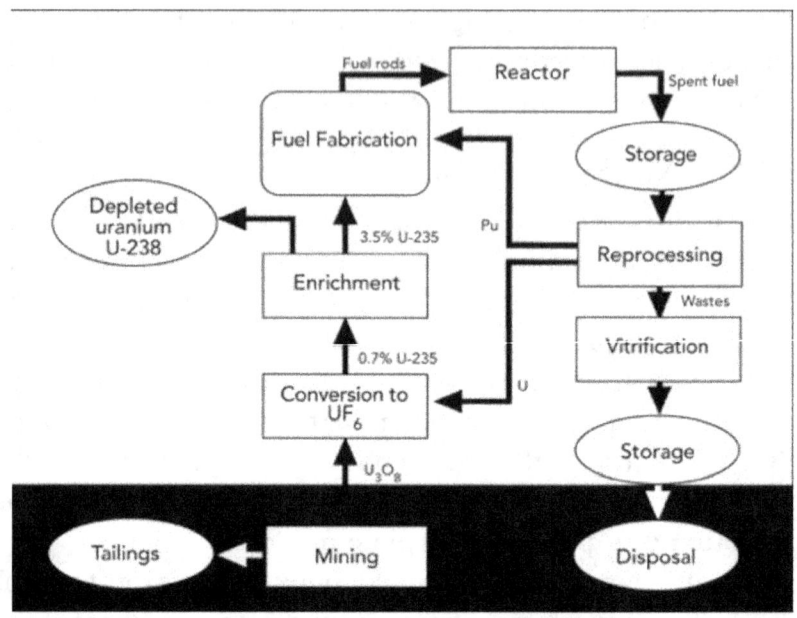

Figure 4.1: *The Uranium Cycle for nuclear power generation.*

to a gas and enrichment, manufacture into fuel elements, burning in a reactor, storage and reprocessing, followed by waste treatment.

The ore is crushed and then finely ground in water slurry to a size that allows separation of the uranium oxide (U_3O_8) from the surrounding waste rock. The slurry is then pumped to a vessel in which the uranium oxide is dissolved (leached) by sulphuric acid. The uranium-bearing solution is then filtered to separate the uranium oxide from the rest of the solids, which are called tailings. The uranium in solution is separated and purified. The tailings still contain a small amount of radioactive material (much less than in the ore as it was originally mined), and are pumped to a dam for drying. Their fine particle size makes the tailings more susceptible to being inhaled and therefore more hazardous. Ideally they should be covered with soil and planted with vegetation, or stored in underground storage areas.

The uranium solution is then treated with ammonia to produce a bright yellow powder called 'yellowcake' – 98% uranium oxide (U_3O_8) that is dried at 700°C and loaded into steel drums for export as a yellow powder. This is the end of the current nuclear cycle in Australia, although a small amount is ultimately enriched abroad and returned as fuel for the research reactor at Lucas Heights in New South Wales. In 2016, Australia produced 7,447 tonnes of yellowcake. The world's leading producer is Kazakhstan followed by Canada. Australia probably occupies third place as it is a higher cost producer. Uranium in the yellowcake produced at the mine contains only 0.72% of the targeted isotope (U235), with the balance being U238. The first step in enrichment is conversion, in which the uranium is purified and converted to a gas – uranium hexafluoride (UF_6).

Enrichment has been achieved by either the older diffusion or later centrifugal processes. In the **diffusion** process, the gas is passed repeatedly through a series of porous barriers. The more common **centrifuge** process causes the slightly heavier U238 to be forced further to the outside of rapidly rotating centrifuges in much the same way as milk and cream are separated in the dairy. The process is repeated over many stages to gradually separate the isotopes based on their very slight mass difference (0.8%). Reactor grade uranium is in the range 3.5-5% U235.

NUCLEAR WEAPONS[23]

Along the way, weapons and reactor grade uranium part company. Weapons grade uranium is enriched to near 100% pure U235. The enriched UF_6 is then reduced to pure uranium metal by the Ames process.[24] The first step of the natural decay of U235 to Th231 is extremely slow as U235 is relatively inactive and is quite safe to handle, with a half-life of 700 million years. It seems an unlikely starting point for a nuclear explosion. If, however, U235 is bombarded with neutrons, the atoms start to become unstable and divide. This called nuclear fission, and U235 is said to be fissile.

> Several reactions occur but this a typical example:
> $$_{92}U^{235} + {_0}n^1 \rightarrow {_{36}}Kr^{92} + {_{56}}Ba^{141} + 3n + energy$$

The three neutrons produced in the fission of U235 then react with another three U235 nuclei to produce another three neutrons, and so on. **The resulting decay products have less total protons than the original U235. They require less binding energy to hold their nuclei together and that energy is released as kinetic energy in the fission fragments.** This is called a chain reaction and occurs instantaneously.

The ideal shape for the U235 is a sphere, which has the minimum surface area for any specific mass. Any reactions that occur near the surface of the sphere of U235 will result in escape of neutrons and slow down the chain reaction. If

---

[23]For an excellent account of the development of the American atomic bombs see Richard Rhodes, *The Making of the Atomic Bomb*, (Simon and Schuster: New York, 1986)

[24]see https://www.ameslab.gov/mpc/the-ames-process-rare-earth-metals 17 Jun 2017

the sphere is too small, the chain reaction will stall. The critical mass is the minimum mass of the sphere that will support a chain reaction. For a U235 weapon the critical mass is a bare sphere of 17 cm and a mass of 52 kg.

The bomb is initiated by having two subcritical masses of U235 such that when the two are forced together they make a spherical mass more than the critical mass. In the uranium bomb dropped on Hiroshima this was achieved by firing one hemisphere into the other; the device was nicknamed 'Little Boy'. It is estimated that only one kg of the uranium fissioned, such was the inefficiency of the device. The plutonium bomb at Nagasaki used an implosion method to forcibly collapse a hollow sphere of plutonium (Pu239), and was nicknamed 'Fat Man'. The process

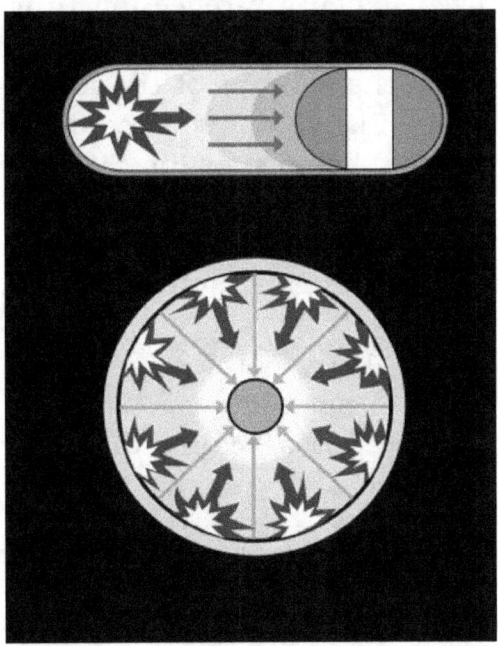

Figure 4.2: *Exploding (top) and imploding (bottom) to make critical mass*

Figure 4.3: *Model of plutonium bomb*

can be improved if neutron-reflecting tungsten carbide is forced onto the plutonium to prevent neutron leakage. Figure 4.2 shows the concept of the first uranium and plutonium bombs. Figure 4.3 is a recreation of the centre of the plutonium bomb showing the upper plutonium hemisphere and the blocks of surrounding tungsten carbide to reflect any escaping neutrons back into the plutonium. These blocks result in a lower critical mass of fissile material.[25,26]

For a semi-fictional view of the story behind the development of the first two nuclear weapons at the Los Alamos New Mexico the TV series 'Manhattan' is an interesting

---

[25]https://en.wikipedia.org/wiki/Critical_mass 15 June 2017

[26]During the assembly of a neutron reflector in 1945 Harry Daghlian became the first known victim of a fatal dose of radiation. He dislodged a neutron reflector brick and the plutonium went critical. He received the fatal dose before the brick could be replaced. See Appendix G

series, particularly the human story in the development of the implosion mechanism.[27]

Adding the atomic weight numbers of the fission products gives a net loss of three neutrons. The lower total atomic mass liberates bonding energy in accordance with Einstein's prediction :

$$E = mc^2$$

...where E is the energy released, m is the mass converted to energy and c is the speed of light. If we could annihilate one kilogram of matter (for example a litre of water) and fully convert it to energy, it would release around 10^{17} joules of energy. For peaceful applications, this amount of energy could supply the power requirements of one million people for a year. In the case of uranium fission, only three neutrons out of a total mass of 236 (1.25%) of each atom can be annihilated and converted to energy.

If this all sounds difficult to comprehend, there are some interesting animations of the nuclear fission process on the internet.[28] [29]

PLUTONIUM: PHYSICIST'S DREAM – ENGINEER'S NIGHTMARE

Plutonium is a metal with the atomic number of 94 that exists naturally in minute amounts as Pu244 (150 neutrons with a half-life 80 million years). Useful amounts are produced artificially from uranium. Pu238 is a power-generating

---

[27]https://dvd.netflix.com/Search?vl=Manhattan 15 June 2017

[28]See for example http://www.visionlearning.com/library/module_viewer.php?mid=59 15 June 2017

[29]See for example http://www.atomicarchive.com/Fission/Fission1.shtml 25 June 2017

alpha emitter (easily shielded) that was used to drive early pacemakers until the development of lithium batteries.[30] Plutonium powered pacemakers require no battery replacement, and some are still in operation. Plutonium is a highly risky material to work with as it reacts with water and oxygen to form self-igniting compounds.

The element was first isolated in 1940 by Glen Seaborg and was produced for the Manhattan Project from 1942 by bombarding uranium with the nuclei (deuterons) of heavy hydrogen (H2) from heavy water. Later, most weapons grade plutonium was produced by bombarding U238 with neutrons from fission. Contrary to what some claim, plutonium was not named after Pluto the god of war, but after the planet Pluto. Between plutonium and uranium on the Periodic Table sits another artificially produced element, neptunium (atomic number 93), completing the symmetry with the periodic table.

The **hydrogen bomb** operates on fusion – the reverse of nuclear fission. Two light elements are fused by a large force, destroying mass and producing even greater amounts of energy. The construction is more complex, with the force being provided by an introductory uranium or plutonium atomic explosion – a bomb within a bomb. The hydrogen bomb was the brainchild of Edward Teller, regarded as a nuclear loose cannon and sometimes seen as the model for Dr Strangelove. The first hydrogen (thermonuclear) bomb was exploded in 1952 by the United States and the second in 1953 by Russia (then the USSR). Britain, France, China, India and Pakistan have also tested thermonuclear

---

[30] http://osrp.lanl.gov/Documents/Pacemaker%20Fact%20Sheet.pdf June 2017

weapons and at time of writing North Korea's capabilities and intentions are uncertain.

Russia's access to nuclear weapons triggered major security alarms and began the arms race between former wartime allies. This alarm was compounded by the USSR's more advanced space technology with the launch of Sputnik. Great Britain, France, and China have also tested thermonuclear bombs. While the first atomic bombs delivered the explosive capacity of 20,000 tonnes of TNT, the hydrogen bomb can deliver destructive capacity in millions of tonnes of TNT. The hydrogen bomb is terrifyingly powerful, but at least the results are cleaner in terms of fallout. By the time that the major powers all had access to nuclear weapons, the world found itself in a tense state of mutually assured destruction (appropriately shortened to MAD). This situation eased to some extent at the end of the Cold war in the 1990s.

NUCLEAR POWER REACTORS[31]

For reactors the enriched uranium hexafluoride gas (UF_6) is converted to uranium oxide powder (UO_2), which is pressed into pellets and sintered under heat to make a 30-gram ceramic pellet. The pellets are then sealed in stainless steel or zirconium tubes and assembled into clusters to form fuel elements for the reactor. Fresh enriched fuel is a faintly radioactive alpha emitter and can be handled quite safely without shielding.

Whereas the objective of a nuclear weapon is to produce an uncontrolled instantaneous release of massive energy,

---

[31]For an easy entry into nuclear reactors see https://www.youtube.com/watch?v=MLJ1ebNcNLM 15 Jun 2017

the aim of a nuclear power station is to produce energy in a controlled and safe manner. There is no way that a conventional nuclear power station can explode like a nuclear bomb or produce weapons grade plutonium or uranium. Reactors use much lower purity nuclear fuel in oxide form rather than the high purity metal required for weapons (typically 96% U235 uranium metal).

As of April 2017, 30 countries worldwide are operating 449 nuclear reactors for electricity generation and 60 new nuclear plants are under construction in 15 countries. Nuclear power plants provided 11 per cent of the world's electricity production in 2014. Thirteen nations rely on nuclear power for at least 25 per cent of their electricity, of which France is the highest with around 70 per cent.[32]

Nuclear reactors work on the principle of nuclear fission, in which neutrons bombard a heavy fissile nucleus (e.g. U235). This nucleus splits and releases two new atoms plus three neutrons to react with further fissile nuclei in a chain reaction. This produces energy in a similar way to nuclear weapons, but at a slower and controlled rate. There are various types of reactor, with similar principles, but with vastly different purposes and detailed design. All nuclear reactors have much in common. A simplified diagram of a typical nuclear pressurised water reactor (PWR) power reactor is shown in Figure 4.4.[33] The reactor (far left) heats water to make superheated steam in a pressurised container, using the heat generated by the nuclear reaction in the core (primary loop). This superheated water then

---

[32]https://www.nei.org/Knowledge-Center/Nuclear-Statistics/World-Statistics 16 June 2017

[33]Nuclear data is from: Bruno Comby, *Environmentalists for Nuclear Energy*, (TNR Editions, Paris:2000), 273

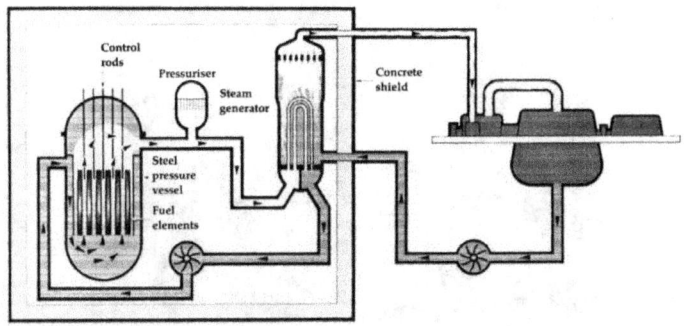

Figure 4.4: *Pressurised Water Reactor (PWR) - Schematic*

heats the secondary circuit to make steam. That steam is piped to drive turbines that produce electricity by turning generators. The steam is then cooled in heat exchangers or cooling towers and fed back into the reactor to be recycled repeatedly in a closed loop. The pressurised water in the reactor is also a closed loop and contained entirely within the reactor. The right-hand side is virtually identical to the turbines and generators of a conventional coal or gas fired power station. Because nuclear reactors use a two-stage heating process, the steam is not as hot as for coal or gas fired boilers, and so the turbines are larger. The condensed steam you see rising from the cooling towers of many power stations (nuclear, gas or coal fired) is from the external cooling water for the heat exchangers and forms no part of the heating process be it from nuclear, gas or coal energy.

The fuel is enriched uranium 235 (as uranium oxide) sealed in zirconium tubes of 1 cm diameter and three metres in length. The fuel is very weakly radioactive and undergoes negligible spontaneous disintegration. When bombarded by neutrons, fissions occur, using the same reaction as occurs in a nuclear weapon, and it produces fission product and

Figure 4.5: *HIFAR – Australia's First Nuclear Reactor*

an average of 2.3 neutrons for the controlled chain reaction ('going critical'). This is the pressurised water reactor (PWR) design, the most common type in current use.[34]

The tubes require gradual replacement over a three-year cycle to maintain efficient reaction. The core is housed in a thick pressure vessel filled with ordinary water. This water acts as a coolant for the core and provides shielding from radiation. It also acts as a **moderator** to slow down fast neutrons. The primary circuit carries a considerable amount of radioactivity. The core also contains control rods holding good absorbers of neutrons such as boron steel or cadmium alloys. When the control rods are fully inserted in the reactor, they absorb all the neutrons and the reaction stops. The output can be controlled by gradually moving the control rods until the desired amount of heat is generated. Think of the reactor as the engine of your car, the control rods as the brakes and the water around the reactor as the radiator.

---

[34]For a more detailed description of the PWR reactors see http://ocw.mit.edu/courses/nuclear-engineering/22-06-engineering-of-nuclear-systems-fall-2010/lectures-and-readings/MIT22_06F10_lec06a.pdf, 25th July 2013

The spent fuel rods are stored under water in special storage tanks on the reactor site to allow their radioactivity to dissipate, and then transferred to storage in dry casks. Spent fuel contains 96% recoverable uranium for new fuel, 1% plutonium and 3% waste. At present, economics favour the use of newly mined enriched uranium over reprocessing spent fuel, but there may soon be strategic, environmental and economic reasons to reprocess all fuel. As all used fuel is usually stored on site, it will be accessible for reprocessing in the future.

The amount of nuclear fuel needed to produce 1000 MW of energy for a year comprises one tonne of U235, mixed with 30 tonnes of U238. Coal fired power stations require the mining, transport, crushing and combustion of 2.7 million tonnes of coal to produce the same amount of energy.[35]

COMPARISON WITH COAL

Steaming coal contains traces of uranium (1.1 grams per tonne), mercury (0.02 grams per tonne), lead (5.5 grams per tonne) and thorium (2.54 grams per tonne).[36] At current burning levels we can expect 3 tonnes of uranium, 100kg of mercury, 15 tonnes of lead and 7 tonnes of thorium to be discharged annually for each 1,000 megawatt of power generation capacity using coal power. These products then find their way into the atmosphere or the by-products of coal ash. Ironically, coal fired power stations produce more local background radiation, toxins and carcinogens than nuclear

---

[35] Similar to two 500MW units at Liddell Power Station, NSW see http://www.macgen.com.au/GenerationPortfolio/LiddellPowerStation.aspx 21st Feb 2008

[36] http://csiro.au/resources/ps2rn.html November 22nd 2007

power stations. For a 1,000 MW power plant the relative annual environmental impact is something like Table 4.6.

Small scale nuclear power reactors have been applied to submarines, (with some spectacular mishaps in the developmental stages) but show potential for small scale generation of electricity for off-grid power in remote urban centres.[37]

Input/Output	Nuclear	Coal Fired (Based on 2/500MW Generators
Fuel	30 T enriched fuel	2.7 million T coal
Carbon dioxide (greenhouse gas)	Nil	2.2 billion cubic metres (5 million tonnes)
Sulphur dioxide (acid rain gas)	Nil	24,000 Tonnes (10million cubic metres)
Nitrogen Oxides (Respiratory irritants)	Nil	13,000 Tonnes (4 million cubic metres)
Airborne Dust	Nil	1,200 tonnes
Solid waste	14 cubic metres of high level waste and 500 cubic metres of intermediate level waste	95,000 Tonnes including 3T uranium, 100 kg of mercury, 15T lead and 7T thorium

Table 4.6: *Relative annual inputs and outputs of nuclear, coal fired and gas fired power stations for a 1,000 MW power station*[38]

AUSTRALIA'S RESEARCH REACTORS

Australia's first nuclear reactor was HIFAR (High Flux Atomic Reactor), a virtual carbon copy of the Harwell

---

[37] http://www.world-nuclear.org/information-library/nuclear-fuel-cycle/nuclear-power-reactors/small-nuclear-power-reactors.aspx Oct 2017

[38] Coal usage and emission data based on Liddell Power Station (see appendix I). Nuclear data is from: Comby, 61-63. For other reference data see Appendix F

reactor in Britain. Construction commenced in February 1956 and the reactor first went critical on 26 January 1958. Full power operation commenced in January 1960. HIFAR was originally built to test materials used in power reactors by subjecting samples to neutron irradiation. The reactor facility was also a source of information and industrial radioactive sources for industries developing new technologies in the post war period. The decision not to pursue a power reactor program in Australia resulted in a gradual change in reactor use over the years towards the production of isotopes for medical and industrial use. The reactor was designed for a thermal production capacity of 25 megawatts, but was used at only 10megawatts and lasted a good deal longer than its design life.

The core contained 25 fuel rods and was about 60 cm x 90 cm (about the size of a small washing machine). The core was cooled with 10 tonnes of heavy water circulating through the core, with the maximum water temperature of around 50 °C. In 2007, HIFAR was replaced by OPAL (Open Pool Australian Light Water Reactor), which is also a research reactor of similar sized core, and twice the thermal output and higher neutron flux density (intensity of neutron production). With the introduction of OPAL, ANSTO has ceased producing industrial radioactive isotopes.

SPENT FUEL AND NUCLEAR WASTE

Spent fuel can be either reprocessed or disposed of. This series of operations is generally called the 'back end' of the nuclear cycle. Spent fuel is still approximately 96% uranium, of which only 1% is fissionable U235. About 1% has been converted to plutonium and the rest is a highly radioactive cocktail of fission products and actinides.[39] These fission products and actinides are called high level waste and need to be isolated from the environment.[40] Nuclear wastes are different to conventional wastes in that they decay over time, whereas many other industrial and commercial wastes such as asbestos, PCBs, industrial acids, lead and mercury retain their toxicity indefinitely. In addition, the management of nuclear waste is the responsibility of those who produce it and involves no social (external) cost to the community.

INDUSTRIAL NUCLEAR WASTE DISPOSAL

The volume of nuclear waste is extremely small by waste management standards. In countries with nuclear power, radioactive wastes comprise less than 1% of total industrial toxic wastes. Nuclear waste has the advantage that it eventually loses its toxicity over time, but the other 99% of non-nuclear hazardous waste remains intractable indefinitely and has hazards of flammability (petrochemicals), corrosiveness (chemicals), toxicity (PCBs and mercury) or reactivity (batteries and explosives).

HIGH LEVEL NUCLEAR WASTES

There are different ways of dealing with nuclear waste in each country, depending on the availability of storage locations, political pressures and the quantities involved. High-level waste in OECD countries comprises 3% of the volume

---

[39] Actinides are those elements from atomic number 89 (actinium) to 103 (lawrencium).

[40] For a more detailed description of nuclear waste, see http://www.world-nuclear.org/information-library/nuclear-fuel-cycle/nuclear-wastes/radioactive-waste-management.aspx 17 June 2017.

of total nuclear waste, but contains 95% of the radioactivity of all nuclear wastes. This waste comprises spent fuel and there is a debate as to whether final disposal of high level waste should be delayed for as long as possible to allow much of the radiation to decay before ultimate disposal. Although the time taken to return to the radioactivity of the original ore can take as much as 10,000 years, half of the radioactivity has dissipated in two years, and 90% has dissipated in twenty years at which point waste management is much simpler. As a longer-term solution, the Australian Nuclear Science and Technology Organisation (ANSTO) has developed a process called SYNROC, in which the radioactive waste is absorbed into the crystallographic structure of artificial rock.[41]

High level wastes also include some longer-term components such as minor actinides and plutonium. After two years, the waste can be transported, and after four years it can be reprocessed. After five years, it can be immobilised in glass (vitrification). The glass is sealed inside corrosion-resistant containers, such as stainless steel, buried deep underground in a stable rock structure and protected from moisture by an impenetrable barrier of bentonite. Final burial takes place after about forty years, when the initial radioactivity has dropped to 0.1% (one thousandth) of its initial activity. There is currently an estimated world stockpile of 10,000 tonnes of high level waste produced by the nuclear industry over the last 50 years, none of which has been permanently buried, still waiting further reduction in activity.[42] This is equiv-

---

[41] For more detail on Synroc, see http://www.synrocansto.com   15 June 2017

[42] Ian Lowe, Reaction Time: Climate Change and the Nuclear Option,

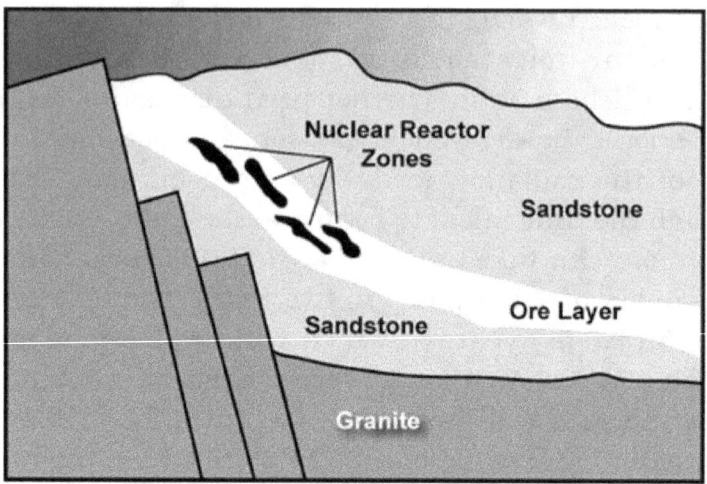

Figure 4.7: *Oklo nuclear reactor*

alent to a volume of 500 cubic meters – equivalent to an 8-metre cube, about the volume of an average house. The volume in vitrified form is much higher. France is 75% reliant on nuclear energy and one estimate of the total volume of French vitrified high-level waste in 2000 was 3,000 cubic metres – about the volume of an Olympic swimming pool.[43]

CASE STUDY IN ACCIDENTAL HIGH LEVEL NUCLEAR WASTE STORAGE

The first known instance of successful nuclear waste management happened naturally one billion years ago see Figure 4.7. At Oklo in what is now Gabon in West Africa in 1972, French researchers found a deposit of uranium that had only 0.44% U235 compared to the normal 0.72%. This implies that some of the U235 had undergone spontaneous

---

Quarterly Essay no 27, (Black Inc, Melbourne:2007), 22
[43]Comby, *Environmentalists*, 87.

nuclear fission at some time in the past when conditions allowed. Fission-produced isotopes of neodymium and samarium were also found. Some samples were found with a U235 concentration as low as 0.29%. Models of the process suggested sustained fission reactions had occurred for about a million years.

The age estimate from cores in the former reactor zones suggests a time between 1.7 and 1.9 billion years ago in the Precambrian era. For U235 (half-life 700 million years) and U238 (half-life 4.5 billion years), this would be sufficient for there to have been a concentration of about 3% for the U235 at the time of the reaction. It is presumed that ground water seeping through the ore served as a natural moderator to slow down the fission neutrons. One of the interesting observations was that the bulk of the fission products seemed to be still in place in their geologic depository after nearly two billion years. This chance occurrence of successfully storing radioactive waste could be taken as evidence that a deliberate attempt to geologically store radioactive waste is feasible.[44, 45]

Storage of high-level nuclear waste requires a sparsely populated area of stable geology in a politically stable environment. Leaders from both sides of the politics in Australia have floated ideas on nuclear waste storage, and have even viewed storage as Australia's international obligation.[46]

---

[44]https://www.youtube.com/watch?v=yS53AA_WaUk 15 Jun 2017(This one is more fun)

[45]http://sti.srs.gov/fulltext/dpms8075/dpms8075.pdf 15 Jun 2917 (for the more serious minded)

[46]See for example a discussion between former Prime Minister Bob Hawke and Tony Abbott - http://www.abc.net.au/am/content/2005/s1469140.htm

We are the place in the world best endowed with geological stability and isolation to store radioactive waste. Waste storage should be openly debated. In 2015 South Australia established a Royal Commission to enquire as to the feasibility of participating in the nuclear fuel cycle. The final report concluded that while Australia was unlikely to implement nuclear power in the immediate future, South Australia could profitably take waste from other countries and store it locally.[47] Another recommendation was the repeal of state and federal legislation prohibitions on development of the nuclear industry in South Australia. These recommendations were abandoned when two thirds of a subsequent citizens' jury reported that it did not want the state to store high level radioactive waste under any circumstances.[48]

INTERMEDIATE LEVEL WASTES

Intermediate level waste is of medium radioactivity and requires some shielding in transport. Intermediate waste includes resins, sludges and chemical residues, as well as contaminated materials from decommissioning old reactors. Some of the materials may be solidified in concrete or bitumen before burial. Intermediate waste comprises 7% of the volume and 4% of the radioactivity of nuclear waste. Waste from the old HIFAR reactor at Lucas Heights is currently still stored on site.

LOW LEVEL WASTE

Low level waste includes such materials as discarded protective clothing and equipment, and is generally

---

[47]https://yoursay.sa.gov.au/system/NFCRC_Final_Report_Web.pdf September 2017

[48]http://www.abc.net.au/news/2016-11-06/sa-citizens-jury-vote-against-storing-nuclear-waste/7999262 September 2017

buried well under ground. The instruments and gloves used in nuclear medicine are typical components of low-level waste. It requires no shielding in transport or handling. To reduce its volume, low-level wastes may be compacted or incinerated before disposal. Low-level waste comprises about 90% of the volume, and about 1% of the radioactivity of all contaminated waste. Some low-level wastes are dumped in the sea, which seems a risky activity until we appreciate that the sea is already by nature a highly radioactive environment. There is an estimated 550,000 million curies ($2*10^{20}$ Bq) of natural radioactivity in the world's oceans, made up of potassium (K40) rubidium (Rb87), radium (Ra226) and polonium (Po210). The total volume of the world's oceans is estimated at around 1.4 million cubic kilometres.[49] This is equivalent to around 140,000 becquerels per cubic metre of seawater. Before giving up surfing, remember that seawater has a high level of absorption, so this natural radioactivity of seawater is mostly absorbed by the water itself.

THE NUCLEAR NON-PROLIFERATION TREATY (NPT)

The prevention of nuclear war is vital to world peace and the preservation of the planet, and no discussion of the political dimension of nuclear energy would be complete without brief mention of the NPT, which had its genesis in 1968 as an international treaty to limit the spread of nuclear weapons. The NPT treaty became effective in Australia in 1973.[50]

At present, there are 191 parties to the treaty including the USA, UK, China, France and CIS (Community of

---

[49] http://hypertextbook.com/facts/2001/SyedQadri.shtml, 15 June 2017
[50] see https://www.un.org/disarmament/wmd/nuclear/npt/ 18 June 2017

Independent States of the former Soviet Union compromising Russia, Kazakhstan and Ukraine). This group of five is known as the Nuclear Weapons States (NWS). The Non-Nuclear Weapons States (NNWS) have promised not to develop nuclear weapons, and to open their nuclear facilities to international inspection at any time. In return for signing, NNWS states will be assisted in developing nuclear energy for peaceful purposes. South Africa developed nuclear weapons in the 1980s but agreed to stop its nuclear weapons program and become a NNWS when it signed the NPT in 1991. Two (Pakistan and India) of the eight known nuclear nations have not signed the treaty. One unconfirmed nuclear nation (Israel) has not signed. North Korea ratified the treaty, violated it and withdrew in 2003. Currently there is serious international concern about North Korea's intentions and the US posturing in response, as well as those of Iran and Iraq. Australia has gone from being a nation that actively sought nuclear weapons on the coat tails of others (as will be discussed in Chapter 7) to one that supports their abolition, albeit with reservations due to our alliance with the USA.[51], [52] While the world nuclear arsenal has decreased since the treaty was implemented in 1970, the number of states possessing nuclear weapons has increased. Australia favours a policy of 'engage not enrage' by negotiating with nuclear states to reduce, rather than imposing blanket bans.[53]

---

[51] Jim Walsh, Surprise Down Under: The Secret History of Australia's Nuclear Ambition, The Nonproliferation Review, Fall 1997, 1

[52] For more about Australian policy see http://dfat.gov.au/international-relations/security/non-proliferation-disarmament-arms-control/nuclear-weapons/Pages/australias-nuclear-non-proliferation-and-disarmament-policy.aspx 17 June 2017

[53] http://www.smh.com.au/comment/we-must-engage-not-enrage-nuclear-countries-20140213-32n1s.html June 2017

The underlying principles of the treaty are non-proliferation, disarmament and the right to peacefully use nuclear technology. Australia is also party to other related conventions concerning such issues as test bans, safety and transport.[54] Other elements of the non-proliferation regime include the Nuclear Suppliers Group (NSG), Nuclear Weapons Free Zones (NWFZ) and the USA-India civil cooperation agreement, which allows India access to nuclear fuel for peaceful uses subject to approval from the NSG. Australia has also negotiated a deal for sale of uranium to India (a non-treaty state), a fact that seems at odds with our commitments to the NPT.

A significant risk to non-proliferation is the existence of undeclared enrichment plants built to produce nuclear weapons. Current Australian legislation prohibits any local enrichment, reprocessing, fuel manufacture or nuclear power plants. One of the ways of controlling proliferation is to control the use and distribution of uranium in any form. Depleted uranium (U238) is used internationally as a radiation shielding material and as a source of plutonium. All users of depleted uranium for shielding purposes in signatory nations are required to account annually for all the metal in their possession as part of their obligations under the NPT.

Some radioactive materials are used in dirty bombs (conventional bombs that disperse radioactive materials such as americium 241, californium 252, caesium 137, cobalt 60, iridium 192, plutonium 238, polonium 210, radium 226 and strontium 90).

---

[54]For a full list of treaties and conventions to which Australia is signatory, see http://www.dfat.gov.au/security/treaties.html 20th August 2007.

The NPT is obviously a cornerstone of controlling the use of uranium and its derivatives. There are continual review conferences on the operation of the treaty since its inception. It is vital that state leaders implement this treaty rigorously, to ensure that radioactive fuel is being used correctly.[55]

The observer is, however, left with the impression that the NPT is wrapped in the best of intentions, but uncertainties remain on the ability of a wilful state to opt out of the treaty or intentionally ignore it. North Korea has been conducting nuclear weapons tests since 2006 and claimed it had successfully tested a hydrogen bomb in 2016. Experts agree that the bombs have been of increasing yield, but have cast doubt on the fact that the 2016 bomb was a hydrogen bomb, given the size of the explosion registered.[56] The international community has been forced to look on and await developments. The big challenge will be to negotiate a way for the North Korean situation to be managed. There is probably a lack of natural justice in nations denying others what they have themselves, but if North Korea has opted out of the NPT they have probably forfeited this natural justice. Watch this space.

---

[55] For more details on the NPT see http://cns.miis.edu 26 June 2017
[56] http://www.bbc.com/news/world-asia-pacific-11813699 27 June 2017

★ ★ ★

Chapter 5:
Natural and Voluntary Radiation

So far we have discussed radiation from isotopes and X-rays produced by humans. There is a large amount of radiation in our environment that impacts on us all day every day. We also use radiation in managing our health, so we need to understand these doses and make sure that the health benefits are not outweighed by the health risks.

NATURAL RADIATION

Our planet subjects us to a constant stream of measurable permanent radiation. This is comprised of several components that affect the body in the same way as artificially produced radiations. Indicative doses for Britain are shown in Figure 5.1.

Australia has a relatively low level of background radiation at around 2 mSv per annum. The American average annual effective dose is 3.6 mSv - mainly due to radon gas. The average worldwide background radiation is

Radiation Source	Radiation Type	Annual Dose (mSv)
Radon in houses	Alpha	0.80
External gamma rays	Gamma	0.36
Cosmic rays	Mainly gamma	0.30
Internal K40 (potassium)	Beta and gamma	0.18
Internal alpha emitters	Alpha	0.16
Internal C14	Beta	0.01
TOTAL		**1.81**

Figure 5.1: *Natural Radiation – Great Britain.*[57]

2.4 mSv per year.[58] About a billion radioactive particles hit your body every day and you will personally emit around 70,000 disintegrations from radionuclides within your body in the ten seconds it takes you to read this sentence. Sleeping with another human being will increase this dose by ten per cent. Natural radiation comes from many sources.

RADON GAS

From Appendix B you will see that radium as Ra226 decays to produce radioactive radon gas – Rn222, a very heavy gas that emits alpha particles. It has a half-life of only of 3.8 days as it decays to polonium 218 by the emission of an alpha particle. Further solid decay products down to lead lodge in the body. Based on the 'Linear No Threshold' (LNT) risk model it is estimated that radon gas

---

[57] J H Fremlin, *Power Production – What are the Risks?*, (Oxford: OUP, 1987), 55

[58] Committee on the Biological Effects of Ionising Radiations, Board of Radiation Effects Research, Commission of Life Sciences, National Research Council, *Health Effects of Exposure to Low Levels of Ionising Radiation: BEIR VII*, (Washington: National Academy Press, 1990), 18

is responsible for the deaths of 1,000 people per year in Britain.[59] Radon gas is concentrated in poorly ventilated areas such as cellars. In the open, the gas is dispersed and is a minor hazard. Radon gas is a relatively low risk factor in Australia.

EXTERNAL GAMMA RAYS

External gamma rays originate from naturally occurring isotopes in the earth's crust and vary with local geological conditions.

COSMIC RAYS

Cosmic rays are a mixture of protons, neutrons, heavy ions and electrons from outside the Earth's atmosphere. The earth's atmosphere blocks many of these particles, but some do penetrate, and they make up as much as 20 per cent of the radiation we receive. Cosmic rays are much more intense at high altitudes, so modern high-altitude air travel increases the exposure to cosmic radiation. At 9,000 metres, the exposure can be as much as 100 times higher than at ground level. Exposure at the poles is twice as high as at the equator. Frequent flyers and air crew are susceptible to cosmic radiation, and it is estimated that air crew travelling 600-800 hours a year on long haul flights will receive an additional 2-5 mSv per year. You will probably receive about 0.2 mSv on a round the world flight. Figure 5.2 shows the gamma radiation dose received by a passenger on a flight between Sydney and Melbourne for an aircraft climbing to 35,000 feet over 18 minutes, cruising,

---

[59] As will be seen later, the LNT model is one of a number of hypotheses and if alternate models are adopted the deaths attributable to radon gas may be far less.

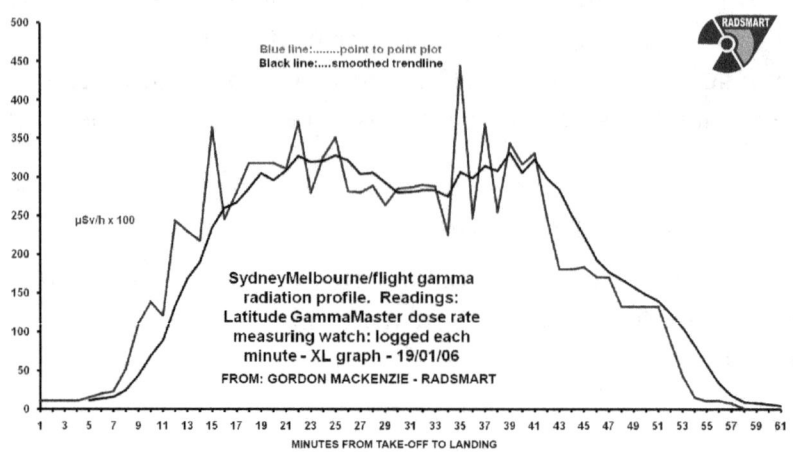

Figure 5.2: *Dose received on a flight from Sydney to Melbourne (courtesy Gordon McKenzie)*

then descending.[60] The estimated additional gamma dose for this flight was 1.9 μSv. The estimated background dose at sea level would have been approximately 0.15 μSv.

Much higher doses of cosmic radiation of around 20 μSv/h are received by astronauts on the International Space Station, and more when outside the space station. On a typical mission, an astronaut would receive around 250 mSv. The space station is shielded to some extent at its normal orbit, but astronauts on the moon's surface would receive even higher doses.

INTERNAL POTASSIUM (K40)

This is a naturally occurring beta emitting isotope that exists in the environment and is taken into the body – usually orally. Potassium is sometimes used in salt substitutes

---

[60]Courtesy Gordon McKenzie of Radsmart Pty Ltd

and may increase the potassium level in the body. It is also a component of many fertilisers and occurs naturally in bananas. You would have to eat a lot of bananas to put your health at risk. There is an unofficial dose unit called the BED (banana equivalent dose). One banana = 0.1 μSv (It's unlikely to catch on).

CARBON 14

C14 is in our bone structure and is used for estimating the age of relics (see earlier in Chapter 3). It has no major influence on our annual dose rate.

OTHER INTERNAL EMITTERS

The body plays host to several traces of radionuclides of uranium, thorium, radium, polonium and tritium.

REGIONAL VARIATIONS

Around the world, the estimates of background radiation vary, but they are usually in the range between 2 and 3 mSv per year. There are many places recording as low as 1 mSv per year and some as high has 10mSv per year. The highest reported location in the world is at Ramsar in Northern Iran, where annual dose rates are in the range 50-150 mSv/yr, and there are recorded annual dose rates of over 40 mSv/year in India, China and Brazil.[61] Probably the most significant high dose affecting a large population is in part of Kerala, Southern India, where the population receives a maximum 50 mSv/yr and an average annual dose rate of over 15 mSv/yr. This is three times the level of

---

[61] http://www.angelfire.com/mo/radioadaptive/ramsar.html 30th June 2017

background radiation at Chernobyl. Background radiation in Australia varies with the geological features – granite in the New England region of NSW emits more radiation than in the plains country. Many of the trace minerals such as thorium in monazite in beach sand along the east coast are radiation emitters.

VOLUNTARY MEDICAL EXPOSURES

In addition to the naturally occurring radiation in the environment, we voluntarily submit ourselves to radiation doses in the expectation that they will provide a benefit in diagnosis or treatment. In the early days of the X-ray industry there was a boom in using radiation in quite pioneering and barnstorming applications that often put the population at risk.

Over the last 60 years, regulation of the medical application of radiation has become increasingly stringent. We can now assume that working in accordance with the regulations, informed professionals and their patients will receive doses no greater than those designated by law. For those of us in the public, however, it is still important to raise awareness. We may protest and enquire about the safety of industrial radiation, but willingly subject ourselves to exposures in our private lives.

For each procedure, a typical effective dose is shown in millisieverts, from 0.02 for a simple chest X-ray to 10.0 for an abdominal CT scan. Certain medical procedures generate relatively high doses, especially if they are repeated. Nuclear medicine has enormous benefits, but these come at a risk. As a rule, diagnostic doses are relatively low risk, but therapeutic doses come at a higher risk in the expectation that the benefit outweighs the risk. The next chapter will try to put a number on that risk.

The object of discussing natural and voluntary radiation is not to scare people. Rather it is to give the role of radiation a sense of perspective. Natural radiation is an inescapable fact of life. In Australia, we are fortunate in our relatively low level of ambient radiation. People in other countries can receive much more. We also receive significant amounts of radiation in diagnosis or treatment, in the expectation that the benefit is greater than the risk we will be exposed to. The next chapter will try to put numbers on that risk.

* * *

Chapter 6:
Human Effects of Radiation

The **Radium Girls** were female factory workers who contracted radiation poisoning from painting watch dials with self-luminous paint. Painting was done by women at three different sites in the United States. The women in each facility had been told the paint was harmless, and subsequently ingested deadly amounts of radium after being instructed to 'point' their brushes on their lips. Some also painted their fingernails, face and teeth with the glowing substance. The paint contained radium 226 and radium 222, which were both alpha emitters and absorbed into the mouth area and beyond. This was the first recorded radiation incident and it showed the harmful effects of radiation. Many of these women died because of their exposure. Less well known are the effects of radiation on early underground uranium miners, who have been studied over the last 30 years.

We now know that radioactivity can be injurious to living creatures. Many of the early workers in radioactivity and X-rays had their lives unnecessarily shortened by not knowing the harmful effects of the materials they were using. Madame Curie is thought to have been such a victim, dying from leukaemia at 67. While this is quite possible it can never be proven either way as we will see later.

In 2016 I spent a day in Hiroshima and saw first-hand evidence of the devastation caused by that first atomic bomb when it was dropped over the city in 1945. Much of the horror brought down on the people was caused by the immediate fire and building collapse. But atomic explosions added longer term radiation effects.

There are two traditionally acknowledged ways in which we can be affected by radiation. They are generally called **acute-deterministic** and **chronic-stochastic (random)**. Acute-deterministic effects are those felt simultaneously with or immediately after high levels of exposure. The other characteristic of an acute effect is that as the dose increases, the effect increases. Sunburn is an acute effect as it is felt almost immediately and **the greater the exposure, the worse it gets**. Chronic-stochastic effects are those that may or may not happen, but **the greater the exposure the greater the PROBABILITY that they will happen.** An effect of smoking can be lung cancer, but not smoking is no guarantee that you will never suffer from lung cancer. Likewise, a heavy smoker may never contract lung cancer, but there is undoubtable evidence that the risk (probability) of lung cancer increases with cigarette smoking.

Many of the residents of Hiroshima would have suffered acute effects from radiation and many would have died from them, but it has not been possible to identify deaths that occurred from acute radiation effects alone, as the destruction of the bomb flattened most buildings within a 3 km radius, and many perished from burns and building collapse. Survivors, however, have been subjected to intense study to record data on the more insidious chronic effects. The relationship between acute and chronic/stochastic effects is shown in Figure 6.1

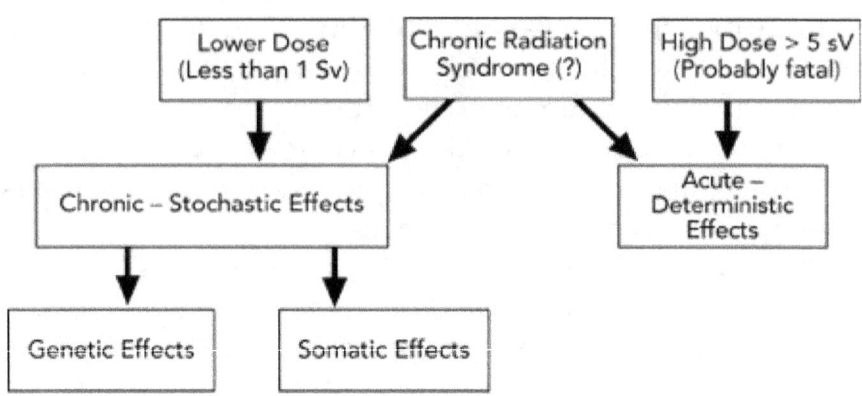

Figure 6.1: *Relationship between somatic, genetic and acute effects.*

INTERACTION OF IONISING RADIATION WITH THE BODY

When radiation enters the human body it can cause chemical changes that can disrupt the way the body works. If the doses are high, there will be massive cell death, organ damage and possible death to the individual. These acute-deterministic effects are caused by the sorts of dose received by those near the centre of the atomic bombs, as well by the firemen at Chernobyl in 1986 and a number of other fatal radiation events. In these instances, the radiation is delivered in large doses, either instantaneously or over a very short period of time.

We will now consider the effects of ionising radiation in decreasing order of severity.

ACUTE-DETERMINISTIC EFFECTS.

Warning: Skip the next two pages if you're squeamish. You are almost certainly never going to have to worry about acute effects, but they must be included to show the whole story.

As mentioned earlier the words 'acute' and 'deterministic' mean different things, but they can be used in combination to best describe the effects of large amounts of radiation on the human body. In this context, 'acute' means effects that would be obvious within days, and 'deterministic' means that those acute effects would be in proportion to the dose received.

Exposure (mSv)	Health Effect	Time to Onset (without treatment)
50-100	Minor changes in blood chemistry	Not noticed
500	Nausea – temporary sterility	Hours
550	Fatigue	Days
700	Vomiting	
750	Hair loss	2-3 weeks
900	Diarrhoea	
1,000	Haemorrhage	
4,000	Possible death	Within 2 months
10,000	Destruction of intestinal lining, internal bleeding and death	1-2 weeks
20,000	Damage to central nervous system loss of consciousness and death	Minutes to days

Figure 6.2: *Likely effects of a large single whole-body dose to humans*[62]

High exposure accidents since 1945 and the Chernobyl accident of 1986 have provided useful anecdotal information

---

[62]http://www.epa.gov radiation/understand/health_effects.html, 20 Feb 2013 Source data is quoted in Rem, and converted to mSv on the basis that 1Rem = 10mSv

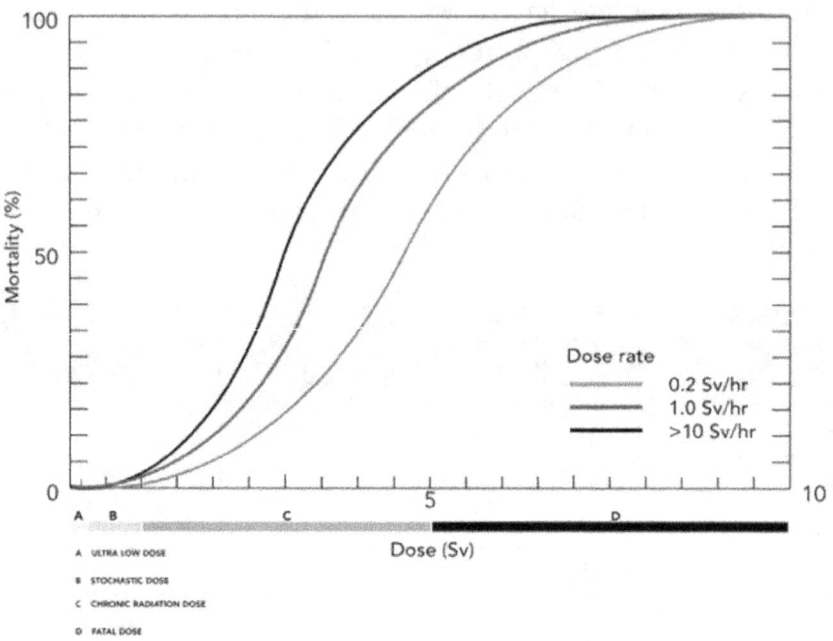

Figure 6.3: *Likely acute effects of a range of radiation doses for various dose rates. High (left curve), medium (centre curve) and low (right curve)*

and the results from both studies are summarised in Figure 6.2 for higher doses. No unambiguous data on dose rate has been possible from the atomic bombs of 1945. These are general guidelines and will depend on the age, gender, health and lifestyle of the recipient. Fatal extreme radiation doses affect the blood, digestive system and nervous system.

This data is shown in another way in Figure 6.3.[63] What this tells us is that:

---

[63] https://en.wikipedia.org/wiki/Acute_radiation_syndrome#/media/File:Death_by_haematopoietic_syndrome_of_radiation_sickness-_influence_of_dose_rate.png 26 Jun 2017

- at a high dose rate of 10Sv/h:
  - 7 Sv total dose means certain death
  - 3 Sv total dose gives a 50% chance of survival
  - 1 Sv total dose is almost certain survival.
- at a low dose rate of 0.2 Sv/h:
  - death is almost certain at 8 Sv total dose
  - death is a 50% probability at 4.5 Sv total dose
  - death is unlikely at 2.5 Sv total dose.
- the risk from exposure increases with dose rate as well as with dose
- this graph falls to zero at around 1 Sv, below which the effects will be primarily chronic-stochastic.

Before getting depressed about this morbid data, remember we are talking about very rare occurrences of extremely high exposures delivered at very high dose rates under exceptional circumstances. One published list of known fatal acute dose accidents is shown in Appendix G, which is at best an approximation.[64]

There have been approximately 100 confirmed fatalities but the French Institut de Radioprotection et de Sûreté Nucléaire (IRSN) estimates there have been as many as 180 deaths since 1945 from Acute Radiation Syndrome (ARS), so a conservative estimate of the number of deaths from ARS is probably somewhere between 100 and 200. The worst event by far was at Chernobyl in 1986. Reports differ, but acute radiation sickness affected an estimated 234 people, of whom 28 died within three months. There were 15 subsequent deaths and the remainder survived.

---

[64]https://en.wikipedia.org/wiki/Acute_radiation_syndrome (28 Jun 2017)

In other incidents, there have been three associated with crime, four have been due to an orphaned (lost or misplaced) radioactive source, four associated with radiotherapy when patients received excessive doses, three with Soviet submarines and one with a non-military power reactor (Chernobyl). Russia/USSR is certainly over-represented, and their data include some political murders. There were no acute radiation deaths from the Three Mile Island or Fukushima incidents.

Fortunately, acute radiation sickness is rare. The more important insidious effects are those from low doses and the chronic-stochastic effects. They are also the most contentious effects.

CHRONIC-STOCHASTIC EFFECTS

At lower doses, the recipient demonstrates somatic effects and later generations demonstrate genetic effects. It has been difficult to obtain data on the probability of cancer in the chronic-stochastic range. It is not possible to carry out deliberate experiments and researchers rely on unforeseen events.

Also, the analysis is extremely long term, as a lifetime is needed to gather meaningful data on groups.

RANDOMNESS AND RISK

Understanding stochastic effects requires an appreciation of randomness. Here are three arbitrary laws of randomness:

> **There is such a thing as randomness.** Forget all about karma, cosmic equalisation, runs of good and bad luck, things happening in threes, phases of the moon, that everything that happens has a cause or somebody else is to blame.
>
> **Some results are impossible to predict.** If you try to predict one throw of a dice you will be wrong five times out of six.
>
> **Random events are predictable in general and unpredictable individually.** If you throw a dice six thousand times, you will get each number about a thousand times.

THE DNA MOLECULE

The double helix structure of the DNA molecule is our individual genetic blueprint. The basic DNA molecular structure can be represented simply as two helixes, each like the rails of a spiral staircase, with sub-molecular links joining the helixes, like the steps in a spiral staircase (See Figure 6.4). There are four types of these sub-molecular bases, which join to make the links, called for short A (adenine), C (cytosine), G (guanine) and T (thymine). The four sub-molecular links form a four-letter alphabet. It is possible to specify the DNA of any living flora or fauna with this string of the letters A, C, G and T in an order that is unique to the individual animal or plant. The string of letters (known as the DNA code) that uniquely defines any individual is about 3 billion characters long.

As we grow, the DNA molecule is continuously dividing and duplicating itself exactly. Unfortunately, if a molecule is damaged, The error will be transferred every time the

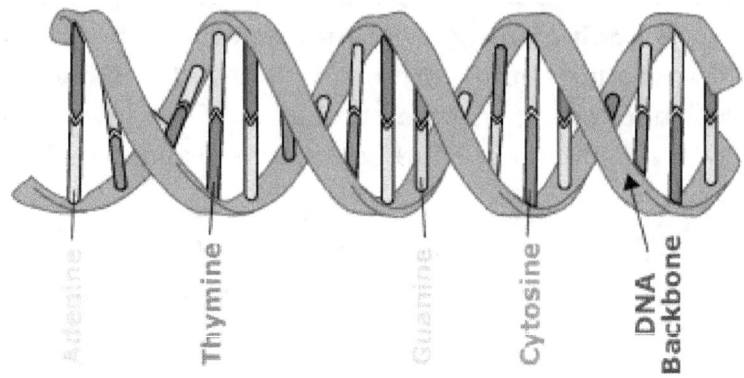

Figure 6.4: *Simplified Model of part of a DNA Molecule*

faulty cells divide until a cluster of damaged cells starts to build up in the body, and this may be the start of a cancer. This error may occur naturally or be triggered by an external factor. The result is that in our lifetime around 40% of us will contract a cancer and half of these cases will be fatal.

Try this website for a few animations of DNA division to help your understanding of cell division: https://www.youtube.com/watch?v=ZZUk0gF_-T4

During growth from foetus to adulthood, cells and the DNA within them are continually dividing – rapidly at first and slowing with adulthood. Cancers may occur spontaneously for no reason or when the DNA data is corrupted by some external factor such as ionising radiation, cigarette smoke, high levels of alcohol or one of the hundreds of other carcinogens. Some cancers may be linked to genetic make-up. A list of some of the known carcinogens identified by the World Health Organisation (WHO) is shown in Appendix E.[65]

---

[65]http://monographs.iarc.fr/ENG/Classification/ 12 June 2017

You will see many familiar items from everyday life, as well as ionising radiation. Another effect is mutation, in which the genetic code is corrupted and passed on to the next generation. Cancer is called a **somatic** effect (occurs in the receiver) and mutation is a **genetic** effect (occurs in a descendant).

> ### THE GENOME BOOK
>
> A useful way of thinking about **DNA** is to think of the human **genome** as a book that describes what you are – down to the colour of your eyes and length of your nose. It is the recipe of how you are built as cells divide and divide again from the moment of your conception until the day you die. It is a rather long book of a billion words – equivalent to 800 Bibles using a four-letter alphabet and is being copied over and over again throughout your life.
>
> This so-called book (**genome**) is divided into chapters, or **chromosomes**. Each chapter contains several thousand paragraphs, or **genes**. Each paragraph (gene) is made up of sentences (**exons**), each separated by spaces (**introns**). These sentences (exons) may be long or short, and together with the spaces (introns) are strung in a sequence along a **DNA** strand. The sentences (exons) use an alphabet of four letters (**bases**) – A,C,G and T to make up words (**codons**). **DNA** is an abbreviation for deoxyribonucleic acid, a self-replicating material in nearly all living organisms which carries the genetic information of that organism.

> A **cell** is the smallest functional unit in a living organism or tissue, and is composed of DNA in its nucleus, which is bound in a membrane.[66]

This rate of cell division is extremely rapid in the developing foetus and in growing children, so the susceptibility to damage in growing infants is much higher than in mature adults. Fortunately, the human body has evolved to tolerate a certain amount of ionising damage, most of which is self-repaired, just as the body self-heals from the cuts, bruises, fractures and scratches we experience in our daily life. Our bodies are continually being bombarded by radiation at the rate of 70 billion hits per day. If the dose is so high that there is either no repair or a faulty repair, it is possible to initiate cancer or pass on a mutated gene to descendants. Just imagine if you received all the cuts, bruises and fractures sustained in your entire life in one day. You would probably not survive. The same is the case with radiation; if you received your entire lifetime environmental and medical X-rays in one day you would be at much higher risk. Figure 6.5 shows some typical doses in the stochastic-chronic range.

Figure 6.6 is a model for interaction of radiation with a normal cell. Incoming radiation interacts with a normal cell, which either self-repairs perfectly, dies or is damaged (mutagenic repair). Error-free repair or death of a cell poses no risk, but a surviving damaged cell may divide and multiply, and become a cancer site. Below 100 mSv the rate

---

[66] I am indebted to Barry Maitland and his novel 'Babel' for this analogy

Typical Stochastic – Chronic Doses

Below **1 Sv (1,000 mSv)**, the **probability** of cancer increases with dose. About 200,000 clean-up workers at Chernobyl received an average of 100 mSv. There is evidence of greater cancer development among those who received 150 mSv or more in a very short time. Reoccupation of the Chernobyl area was allowed when the estimated **lifetime** radiation dose had dropped to 350 mSv. That is, the current dose rate is now approximately 5 mSv per year.

50 mSv is the highest dose allowed by regulation in any one year of occupational exposure. (Note that the average dose must not exceed 20 mSv/yr over five years). It is also the minimum natural background radiation received by residents of Ramsar, Iran.

20 mSv/yr averaged over five years or more is the legal limit for radiological personnel, workers in the nuclear industry and medical workers (who are all closely monitored).

15 mSv/yr is the average background radiation in parts of Kerala, India.

10mSv/yr is the maximum permissible dose received by an Australian uranium miner.

3-5 mSv/yr is the actual occupational dose rate received by uranium miners and radiation workers in Australia and Canada.

3 mSv/yr (approx) is the typical background radiation from natural sources in North America, including an average of almost 2 mSv/yr from radon in air.

2 mSv/yr (approx) is the typical background radiation in Australia from natural sources. The range of typical dose rates on Earth varies between 1 and 10mSv/year.

0.3-0.6 mSv/yr is a typical range of dose rates from medical sources.

Figure 6.5: *Lower Doses of Ionising Radiation*

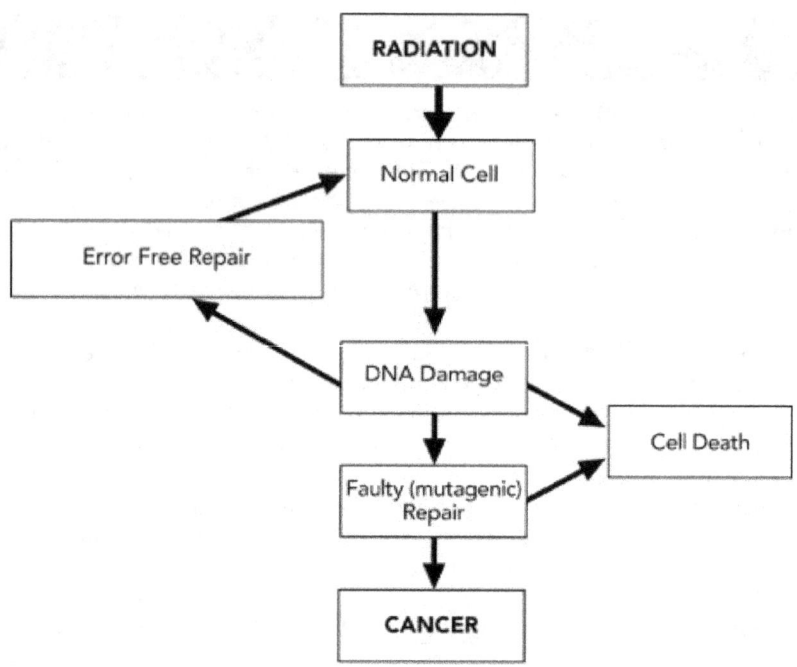

Figure 6.6: *The interaction of radiation with a normal cell.*

of faulty mutagenic repairs is small.[67] This rate increases, however, with dose and dose rate. Within the population there is considerable genetic variability in sensitivity to ionising radiation.

There are also **genetic effects** when reproductive organs are exposed to ionising radiation. There may be temporary or permanent sterility in some cases, and possible hereditary effects transmitted to our descendants. It takes generations to study these genetic effects, but we are now beginning to better understand them.

---

[67]Maurice Tubania, Dose-Effect Relationship and Estimation of the Carcinogenic Effects of Low Doses of Ionising Radiation: the Joint Report of the Acedemie des Sciences (Paris) and of the Academie Nationale de Medecine, Int Jnl Radiation Oncology Biol Phys, Vol 63 No 2, 316 (2005).

LIFETIME CANCER RISK FOR A WHOLE POPULATION

Authoritative and well-researched data on cancer and the genetic effects of these lower doses is contained in the publications of the American Biological Effects of Ionising Radiation (BEIR) Committee and the World Health Organisation (WHO). Results for both of these organisations are similar, except that WHO results are reported as a range rather than a single number.

The probability statistics quoted in this chapter are from the BEIR VII report of 2006.[68] Approximately 20 per cent of all deaths in OECD countries result from cancer. The number of cancers attributable to low level radiation is a small fraction of the total number that occur due to pure chance and other carcinogens. Cancers caused by radiation normally have no markers that distinguish them from those produced by other causes, so cannot be isolated for special study. To determine the effect of a specific level of radiation it is necessary to compare the cancer rates in the **exposed** population to the cancer rates in the **general** population and see whether there is a measurable difference. These studies are complicated by the fact that our population is ageing, and people are living longer. It is reasonable to expect that there would be a natural increase in the incidence of cancer as medical science delays mortality from other causes such as heart disease, infection and trauma.

The principal data available has been based on 75,991 survivors of Hiroshima and Nagasaki who have been

---
[68]Board on Radiation Effects Research, Division of Earth and Life Sciences, National Research Council, Health Risks from Exposure to Low Levels of Ionising Radiation – BEIR Phase 2, (National Academy Press: Washington, 2006), 1-18.

monitored since 1945. As these people survived, it was possible to get stochastic data and their health could be monitored over time. Of those survivors, 34,272 were so far from ground zero that they received a negligible estimated dose (less than 5mSv). This group has acted as the control group for the studies. This left 41,719 whose estimated dose was greater than 5 mSv.

Radiation exposure has long been associated with most forms of leukaemia, as well as cancers in organs such as lung, breast and thyroid gland, but not with certain other organs such as the prostate.[69] The BEIR VII data tells us that at current cancer rates, an additional dose of one milli-Sievert to a large population corresponds to a likelihood of an additional 11 persons per 100,000 contracting a cancer in their lifetime, of which six would be fatal. This figure can be compared with the normal incidence of 41,910 per 100,000, of which 20,420 would be fatal. (See Appendix H for the calculation of additional risk factors.) Note that these risk factors are a worst-case scenario and approximate only, as the risk would depend on age and health at the time of exposure and other factors.

The take home message of this data is that if we assume what is called the 'Linear No Threshold Model' (LNT – defined in the next chapter) we can produce a table of the estimated effects of various levels of radiation doses and their additional risk of lifetime cancer as shown in Figure 6.7.[70]

---

[69]Report of the United Nations Scientific Committee on the Effects of Atomic Radiation to the General Assembly, http://www.unscear.org/docs/reports/gareport.pdf 2nd June 2007

[70]Based on data from BEIR VII Report (Table ES-1), 15.

Lifetime Cancer Risk per 100,000								
Dose (mSv)	0	1	5	10	50	100	500	1,000 (1 Sv)
Base Cancer Cases	41,910	41,910	41,910	41,910	41,910	41,910	41,910	41,910
Extra cases due to dose	0	11	57	114	568	1,135	5,675	11,350
Total cases	41,910	41,921	41,967	42,024	42,478	43,045	47,585	53,260
Base Cancer deaths	20,420	20,420	20,420	20,420	20,420	20,420	20,420	20,420
Extra deaths due to dose	0	6 (0.006%)	29 (0.03%)	57 (0.06%)	285 (0.3%)	570 (0.6%)	2,850 (2.9%)	5,700 (5.7%)
Total deaths	20,420	20,426	20,449	20,477	20,705	20,990	23,270	26,130

Figure 6.7: *Estimated effect of whole body radiations for a single dose based on the Linear no Threshold (LNT) model at a conservative risk level of 5.7% per Sievert. Risk for slow doses would be considerably lower. Note that this data applies to cancer risk and at doses between 500 and 1,000 mSv there would be increasing acute effects such as nausea, vomiting, hair loss, diarrhoea, and even haemorrhage.*

WHAT THIS TABLE TELLS US:

- It is estimated that there are 41,910 people per 100,000 (41.9%) in OECD countries contracting cancer of some sort in their lifetime. Of those, 20,420 (20.4%) will die due to cancer.
- The cancer rate is expected to increase anyway as the population ages and medical developments extend life. Other causes of death will diminish, or to put it more bluntly we are running out of other things to die from.
- The 'Extra cases' and 'Extra deaths' rows of the table estimate how many cases and deaths will be attributable to radiation doses ranging from 1 mSv (11 extra cases and 6 extra deaths) to 1,000 mSv (11,350 extra cases and 5,700 extra deaths). By way of confirmation, the United Nations Scientific Committee of the Effects of Radiation (UNSCEAR) reports the lifetime risk of death due cancer in the range 4.3-7.2 per cent per Sievert.[71] Another way of expressing this as an extra cancer risk of 11 per cent per Sv for contracting cancer and 6 per cent per Sv for mortality from cancer due to ionising radiation. At 1,000 mSv we are starting to approach the acute/deterministic area of radiation effects, and the recipient would be feeling other effects such as nausea, diarrhoea and vomiting (see Figure 6.3). This is similar to the distress experienced by patients in radiotherapy treatment.
- The data on which this was developed is by its nature based on estimates, and there is debate that the relationship between dose and risk is not as simple as it looks, and a bit of radiation might be good for you. But that's what the next chapter is about.

---

[71] *Report on the United Nations Scientific Committee on the Effects of Atomic Radiation*, Fifty-ninth session (21-25 May 2012) A67/46, p 12

Importantly – what this table does not tell us is that the greatest risk of damage is during the formative years of development, reaching 15 per cent per Sv in an adolescent, falling to 1 per cent per Sv for a 70-year-old.[72] It also does not account for the genetic variation between families and population groups. It has become more common for women with a history of breast cancer in their ancestors to have breast surgery in anticipation of the risk of contracting cancer. Ashkenazi (Central European) Jews are descended from a relatively small gene pool and are recognised as having a higher probability of breast and ovarian cancer in women, as well as breast and prostate cancer in men.[73]

CHRONIC RADIATION SYNDROME (CRS)

There is a broad range of effects from highly concentrated doses (5 Sv and above) that are unambiguously acute and usually fatal, down to relatively small doses (say less than 100 Sv), where the effects are unambiguously stochastic. Western studies have focussed on these extremes. In the 1950s, Russian experience at Techa River and the Kyshtym contamination led them to identify symptoms they called Chronic Radiation Syndrome, where doses up to 1.5 Sv were received at dose rates 0.1 Sv/year. The result was 'a constellation of health effects that occur after months or years of chronic exposure to high amounts of ionising radiation'[74] and showed deterministic effects. The symptoms seem

---

[72]http://www.imagewisely.org/Imaging-Modalities/Computed-Tomography/Imaging-Physicians/Articles/Ionizing-Radiation-Effects-and-Their-Risk-to-Humans June 2017. This is from the American College of Radiology but makes intuitive sense Jun 2017

[73]https://www.fredhutch.org/en/events/cancer-in-our-communities/ashkenazi-jewish-communities.html (26 June 2017)

[74]https://en.wikipedia.org/wiki/Chronic_radiation_syndrome

to point to a spectrum between the acute and stochastic effects recognised in Western countries. There have been no similar events in Western countries to draw attention to it. Further studies may fill in the blanks between doses of 1 and 5 Sv. In this CRS range, adverse effects accumulate faster than the body's ability to self-repair, and the effects depend on the genetic makeup and health of the victim as well as the dose rate and radiation mix.

POST SCRIPT

Although we regard the speed limits posted on our roads as arbitrary 'safe' speeds to travel, they are no guarantee of your safety. Bridget Driscoll was Britain's first motor vehicle victim. While crossing the grounds of the Crystal Palace in London in 1896, she was struck by an automobile described as proceeding at a reckless pace – 'like a fire engine'. The actual speed was 4 miles per hour (6.4 km/h). The best that the traffic legislators can do is to develop speed limits that are reasonable compromises between safety and practicality. To achieve absolute theoretical safety on the roads would be to abandon all motorised transport and limit pedestrian travel to a slow walk, and that would have its own risks. Similarly, the best that the radiation legislators can do is to develop dose limits along similar lines. A parallel philosophy applies to a driver's blood alcohol – adherence to a legal limit is no guarantee of safety. Different societies make different value judgments.

Just remember – around 0.64 % of the population will die in a motor accident.

★ ★ ★

Chapter 7:
Effects of Small Doses

IS THERE A 'SAFE DOSE'?

*You can show that something is definitely dangerous,
but not that it's definitely safe*

(Tom Standish)[75]

As we come down the level of severity of radiation exposure from catastrophic to everyday, do we ever reach a 'safe' level of radiation? The simple answer is 'a rock-solid maybe'. The regulators have set legal limits, but there is no certainty that exceeding those limits will be detrimental, or that staying within them will protect you from any ill effects from radiation.

There is no official definition of high and low doses, so at the risk of repetition, we will define them as follows:

> **Fatal doses** are those doses greater than 5 Sv (5,000 mSv) – probably fatal.
> **Ultra high doses** are those between 3 Sv and 5 Sv (1,000–5,000 mSv) and are possibly fatal.

---

[75] John Brockman (ed) This Will Make You Smarter Transworld Publishers (2012, London) 281

Very high doses are those between 1 Sv and 3 Sv (1,000–3,000 mSv) serious acute effects and possibly fatal.

High doses are in the range 100–1000 mSv temporary acute effects and with possible chronic effects.

Low doses are in the range 10–100 mSv.

Ultra-low doses are in the range 0–10mSv (around natural background).

As a user of radioactive materials for all my working life, the most frequent questions I was asked was 'What is a safe dose?' or the more immediate practical question 'how far away should I stand?'. There is no right answer to these questions.

In the last chapter, we referred to the LNT (Linear No Threshold) model, that which presumes a proportional (linear) relationship between dose and effects.

WHAT HAPPENS AT VERY SMALL DOSES?

- The 'linear-no threshold' (LNT) model assumes that if we know the risk at a certain dose and assume that the risk from zero dose is zero, we can use these data to construct a straight line (linear) graph of the risk against the dose. It is further assumed that ANY dose has a risk, which can be calculated from the graph. (See the solid black line in Figure 7.1).
- The dashed-dotted line is the same type of LNT behaviour for a low dose rate. Low dose rate is less damaging than high dose rate.
- There is also a linear model with threshold (dotted line) that proposes that there is a radiation threshold necessary to pose any risk.

- Between these is linear/quadratic model (dashed line) with a 'sort of' threshold. If we could prove and specify a threshold dose, legislation would be very simple.

LINEAR, QUADRATIC OR THRESHOLD?

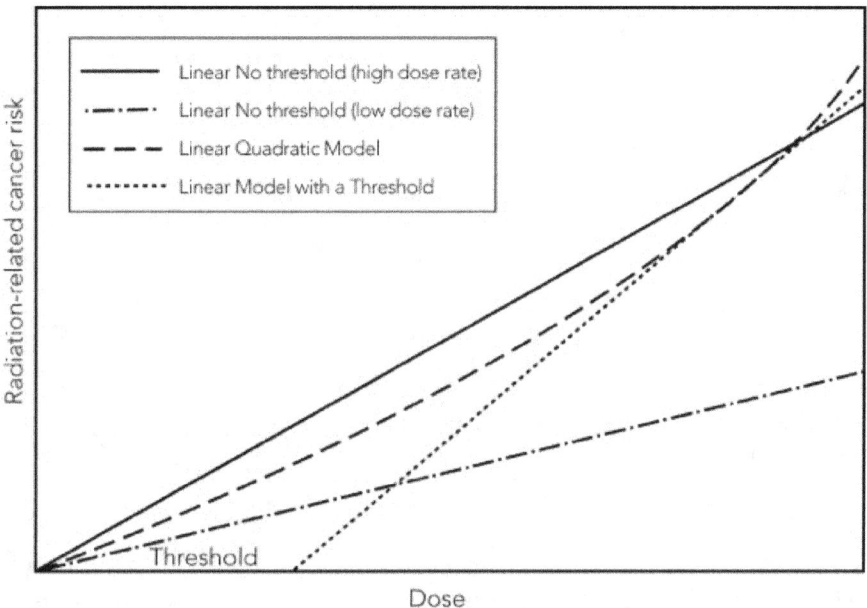

Figure 7.1: *Models of the effects of low level doses of radiation*[76]

As mentioned earlier a controlled experiment to determine this data is not possible, and we rely on data painstakingly collected over many years from unpredictable events like Hiroshima, Nagasaki, Three Mile Island, Chernobyl and Fukushima. While we can draw nice theoretical graphs like Figure 7.1 as models, the actual results

---

[76] From Health Risks from Exposure to Low Levels of Ionizing Radiation: BEIR VII Phase 2 (2006), 7 http://books.nap.edu/openbook.php?record_id=11340&page=7

produce a wide scatter of data points as shown in Figure 7.2 from the BEIR report.

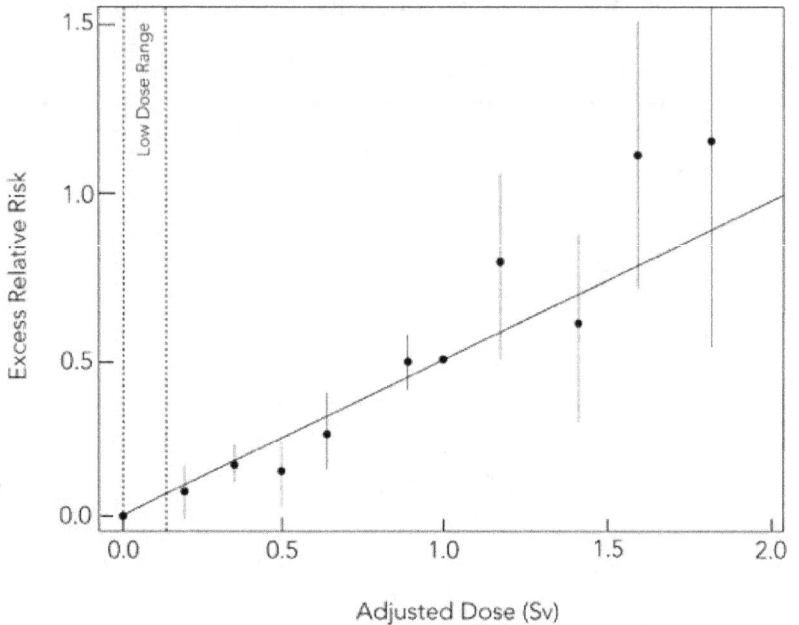

Figure 7.2: *Actual risk-dose correlation for ionising radiation.*[77] *The graphed line is a curve of best fit based on the Linear No Threshold Theory. The vertical lines through each data point show the uncertainty of the data.*

There are significant factors that can contribute to the uncertainty in predicting risk such as:

- transferring results from one population to another
- interpolation of high acute doses to low chronic exposures
- extrapolation of low and high dose rate exposures

---

[77]BEIR VII, 248.

- variations on photon energy
- background doses in the population under study.

The 'Low Dose Range' at the bottom left hand corner of Figure 7.2 is the area of low doses up to 100 mSv, and contains only one data point. The principal relationship shown on the graph is derived from highly scattered data (represented by dots) derived from highly scattered ranges of results (represented by the vertical lines through each data point). The resulting Linear No Threshold relationship (LNT – solid line) has been derived using statistical analysis of scattered data. It is worth noting that in the data for doses up to 600 mSv (0.6Sv) all data points fall below the statistically derived LNT line of best fit. This is the model used most widely by the radiation protection industry in estimating risk. It errs on the side of safety. One factor that is not considered is the age at which the dose is received. Earlier it was noted that lifetime dose effect is much higher if the dose is received up to puberty and much lower if received in old age.

Regulators currently adopt the conservative conclusion of BEIR VII that:

'...current scientific evidence is consistent with the hypothesis that there is a linear, no threshold dose-response relationship between exposure to ionising radiation and the development of cancer in humans.[78]*'*

---

[78] BEIR VII, 15

LIVING WITH RISK

In 1825 George Stephenson, a self-educated colliery mechanic, saw a future in railways. He struggled for recognition while addressing a committee of the British House of Commons. He withstood sneers, interruption and ridicule at the concept of a locomotive travelling at 12 miles per hour (20 km/h). He withstood protracted hostile cross-examination, particularly regarding the safety of the proposed railways. Stevenson's Chernobyl moment came when a man subsequently found to be 'in liquor' overloaded the safety valve and was killed, an accident that would not have happened had procedures been followed.[79]

By the end of the nineteenth century, railways traversed most countries in the world, clearing the way for the next great innovation – the heavier than air machine. By the end of the twentieth century, these could carry over 400 passengers around the world in a day, stopping only once to refuel. Not only that, but we now have our own motorised capsules that give us such individual freedom of movement, an opportunity to kill or maim each other, clog our roads and debase our environment.

Motor travel is a fundamental part of modern life. But motor travel is a risky activity that keeps parents up at night and makes work for ambulance services and emergency departments in our hospitals. We have become inured to the risk despite our best efforts to improve road safety.

---

[79]Fred Hoyle and Geoffrey Hoyle, Commonsense in Nuclear Energy, (Freeman: San Francisco, 1980), 77-79.

ROAD SAFETY IN AUSTRALIA – RISK MANAGEMENT

In Australia, there are 8 road deaths per 100,000 people every year, resulting in the death of around 1,600 Australians annually. Very few people have not had their lives touched by the loss of a friend or relative in a road accident. Over a lifetime of 80 years, 640 people per 100,000 (0.64%) will die on the roads. This is a similar risk rate as the entire population receiving a single dose of 100 mSv and is similar to the dose received by the Chernobyl clean-up workers.

At this rate, during our average lifetime of 80 years, 128,000 people will die on our roads, with up to half a million maimed, disabled or otherwise traumatised. Happily, the annual rate of road fatalities has decreased from 30 per 100,000 in 1970 to the current Figure of 8 per 100,000. This is a reduction of nearly 75%, achieved by many measures that will be familiar to everybody. These include risk management strategies such as improvements to roads, separated dual lane highways, major roads by-passing towns and suburbs, road shoulder sealing, eliminating known dangerous 'black spots', use of audible edge-lining, and removal of roadside hazards. There have also been changes to vehicles by the application of Australian Design Rules, including child restraint anchorages and seats, head restraints, airbags, and increased vehicle impact resistance and roll-over strength. Casualties have been mitigated by legislation requiring the fitting and wearing of vehicle seat belts, and motor cycle and bicycle helmets. There have also been initiatives against drink-driving such as random breath testing and public education campaigns, not to mention improved post-accident treatment. Other enforcement has been aided by improved technology such as red light and speed cameras.[80] It was seat belts and random breath testing that played the major role in reducing road deaths.

We are left with the prudent conclusion that all radiation has some risk, even if individual exposures cannot be linked to outcomes.

LEGISLATION FOR MANAGING RADIATION RISK

Health legislation has followed the conclusion of accepting the most conservative (linear) model for the present, and has placed limitations on the allowable annual dose rate for workers and the general public. Legislation for absolute safety (zero dose) would result in impractical limits. Of course, this will never happen, and we will continue to live with radiation, just as we do with every other part of our lives that contains a risk. Legislation tries to assist in the risk management by establishing limits. Typical measures include licensing organisations or individuals to own and operate X-ray equipment and use radioactive isotopes. There is a mandatory personal monitoring regime for all radiation workers that tracks their dose and health records, establishment of safe working procedures and the compulsory use of monitoring instruments.

Safe working procedures are required to ensure that radiation workers and the public do not receive excessive doses in the workplace. Australian jurisdictions have followed the International Commission for Radiation Protection (ICRP)

---

[80]Road fatalities and injury rates, Australia Bureau of Statistics 1301.0 - Year Book Australia, 2005.

guidelines and have progressively decreased maximum permissible dose levels (MPD) since 1934 (See Figure 7.3). Radiation workers are now successfully working well below maximum permissible dose limits, which are now 40% of what they were in 1977, 13% of what they were when I entered the industry in the 1960s, and 4% of what they were when the baby boomer generation started. The maximum dose for members of the public is one twentieth of that for a radiation worker.

Period	Max Dose[81] (mSv/Yr)
Pre 1934	No limit
1934–1950	500
1950–1977	150
1977–1991	50
1991–present	20

Figure 7.3: *Change in maximum permissible whole body dose (MPD) over time*

GENETIC EFFECTS

If the damage occurs in the testes or ovaries, then hereditary effects in descendants may become apparent. No first-generation hereditary effects were observed amongst Hiroshima survivors. The studies included 75,000 births, of which 38,000 had at least one parent who was exposed to radiation, with no significant variation in still births, birth weight, congenital abnormalities, infant mortality, childhood mortality, leukaemia or gender ratio.[82] Genetic

---

[81]Maximum dose per year averaged over five years with a maximum of 50 mSv in any year.
[82]BEIR VII, 92.

effects need to be studied over generations, and much of the data has been from a combination of sources, including the study of human beings and laboratory animals. Based on other studies, the ICRP has estimated a risk factor of 200 new-borns with genetic defects per 100,000 live births for each Sievert effective dose, compared to a cancer mortality of 5,700 per 100,000.

CANCER CLUSTERS - THE MYSTERY OF ABC BRISBANE

In 2006 an extraordinarily high incidence of disease occurred among employees of the Australian Broadcasting Commission (ABC) in Toowong, Brisbane. Over a period of thirteen years, sixteen female staff members contracted breast cancer – a rate more than six times the national average. Despite extensive testing of the site, no carcinogenic agent was detected that could explain this level of cancer incidence among the staff. Despite the lack of an identifiable cause, the entire Toowong office was relocated in 2007.

The cause of the ABC cluster remains unexplained, and such cases raise considerable difficulties for employers wanting to behave ethically.[83] The ABC closed the office as in their view the anxiety surrounding an unresolved cluster could be as harmful as the possible carcinogen itself. There have also been unresolved clusters at Milpera in Queensland. Clusters usually involve abnormally high incidence of cancer **of a particular type**,

---

[83]http://www.theaustralian.com.au/business/media/abc-cancer-cluster-still-a-mystery/news-story/5f89a41d884a4c7a56c5bf9919d769b7 (27 June 2017)

rather than across the board cancers, and need the support of an underlying hypothesis of a carcinogenic agent such as ionising radiation, asbestos, cigarettes or heavy metals.[84]

In the case of the ABC Brisbane there was no underlying hypothesis, but if the staff members had been working in (or near) nuclear medicine or nuclear energy facilities, or living in parts of Hunters Hill in Sydney, the temptation to make ionising radiation the carcinogenic culprit would have been irresistible.[85] In an ironic twist, when the ABC came to build new premises, the new site was found to contain soil contaminated with radioactivity, causing cancellation of the new construction contract. In December 2008, the final report issued to the ABC concluded that the incidence of breast cancer at the ABC in Brisbane could not be attributed to the level of ionising radiation at the site.

A 2012 study of cancer cluster investigations in the USA over the last 20 years looked at 428 of 567 reported clusters. The study concluded that of the reported clusters, 87 per cent of cases could not be classified as having a true increase, and in only one case could a link be established between the cluster and a carcinogen.[86]

---

[84] Professor Bernard Stewart, Health Report, ABC Radio National, 26th November 2007.

[85] In 2008 a NSW Government Commission investigated the effects of radioactive waste left after the closure of a uranium-processing site that had operated from 1911-1915 in Hunters Hill, a suburb of Sydney. At present the ultimate disposal of the material is still a matter of debate

[86] Critical Reviews in Toxicology: Cancer Clusters in the USA . What do the Last 20 Years Tell Us http://informahealthcare.com/doi/pdf/10.3109/10408444.2012.675315 15 June 2017

> **THE VAGARIES OF CHANCE:**
>
> In 2013, Ashton Agar scored 98 runs in his test cricket debut batting at number 11, an event that had never occurred in test cricket and will probably never happen again – but it happened, and Agar did not play another Test Match for four years.

AN ALTERNATIVE VIEW OF LOW RADIATION DOSE EFFECTS

The risk model discussed so far is based on the traditional LNT (liner no threshold) hypothesis that **all** ionising radiation:

- has a non-zero probability of causing DNA damage
- is cumulative in its effect
- has the same effect, irrespective of dose rate.

There are some more recent ideas that challenge the LNT model and question the established cumulative and dose rate assumptions, and even entertain the counter-intuitive view that a small amount of ionising radiation might be good for you.

Our species has been evolving for more than a million years. A quarter of a million years ago, when our ancestors left Africa to colonise the world, they evolved to breathe their local air and drink their local water. In Australia and many other countries, we are fortunate in the quality of our water, and bottled water is more a fashion statement than a necessity of life. Nonetheless, our water is far from pure, and we have evolved to tolerate and even depend on the impurities to the extent that drinking ultra-pure water can be harmful to our health, just as drinking contaminated water can harm us.

The Linear No Threshold relationship (LNT – solid line) has been derived using statistical analysis of scattered data and is but one possible interpretation of the data. At present, the LNT hypothesis is neither proven nor disproved but remains the model of choice. In Figure 7.2, five of the six data points below 1 Sv (1000 mSv) lie below the LNT line. While of great use in uncomplicated administration and enforcement of radiological protection, the LNT model is not necessarily based on unambiguous science, and while it may be a useful guide for setting safety guidelines, the LNT model is of doubtful value in estimating real life risks.

TECHA RIVER STUDY

There was a rare opportunity to study medium level effects in the Techa River region in the Ural Mountains in Russia. There were significant risks to workers and population downstream from a plutonium enrichment plant on the Techa River after its establishment in 1948 for the Soviet Union's atomic weapons programme. Many in the population received doses of gamma and beta radiation up to 0.4 Gy (400 mSv) at relatively low dose rates from liquid wastes released into the river. This population has shown an increase in cancer response that may only follow the LNT model at higher levels.[87] Experts are not united for doses below 0.2 Gy (200 mSv) for which all results fall below the LNT model. There is a strong suggestion of a change in response behaviour below 200 mSv. (See Figure 7.4).

[87]Krestinina, L Y et al Solid cancer incidence and low dose-reate radiation exposures in the Techa River cohort 1956-2002, Int J Epidemiol, 2007, Oct 36(5), 1038.

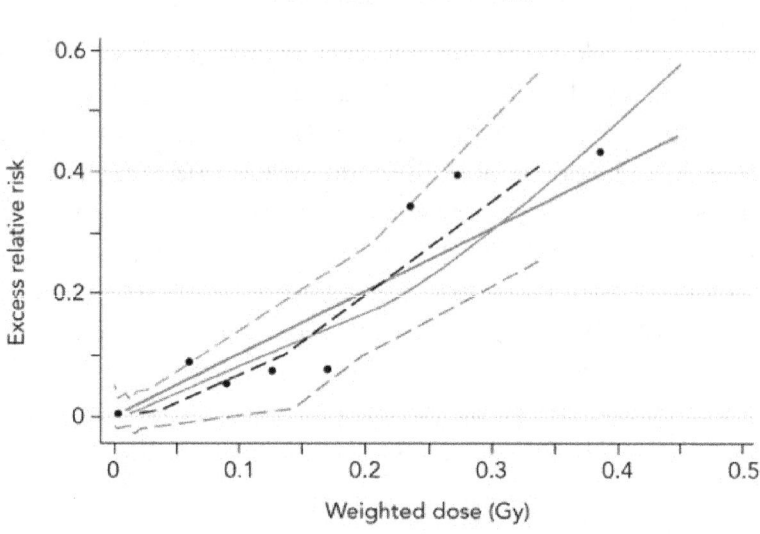

Figure 7.4: *Krestinina et al. Solid cancer incidence dose response in the Techa River study and attempts to fit the data. Note the different response above 0.2 Gy (200 mSv). (The graph lines show attempts to fit the data to various models)*

LESSONS FROM HIGH BACKGROUND RADIATION AREAS (HBRAS)

It is useful to study HBRAs to determine whether the cancer rates are in fact higher than elsewhere, and research has been done in these areas.[88] Some investigations of HBRAs have reported 'lack of ill effects' and lower effects than predicted by the LNT model.[89] There are, however some practical problems in drawing meaningful conclusions from such

---

[88] http://www.iaea.org/inis/collection/NCLCollectionStore/_Public/34/086/34086353.pdf (27 Jun 2017)

[89] http://www.inderscience.com/search/index.php?action=record&rec_id=12016&prevQuery=&ps=10&m=or 2nd July, 2008. http://www.angelfire.com/mo/radioadaptive/ramsar.html 2nd November 2007

data. There may be an adaptive response from people who have lived a long time in a higher radiation environment. The sample sizes are smaller as the populations are relatively low in the most heavily exposed areas; large sample sizes are needed for reliable conclusions.

There is also high dose variability in the affected areas. This makes it difficult to ascribe an average dose to population groups. The four nations involved have variable public health measures and records, and the demographic characteristics as well as lifestyles of each area studied are different. Furthermore, there are different standards of living and life expectancies between populations. Cancer is much more common in developed countries due to the eradication of much of the diseases such as cholera, malaria, whooping cough and measles that had previously resulted in much lower life expectancy. Added to this is the greater availability in more developed countries of drugs for the control of infection. The most promising area for study appears to be in Kerala India, with a population of 30 million, where the population receives a maximum 50 mSv/yr and an average annual dose rate of over 15 mSv/yr. To date there has been insufficient evidence to either confirm or deny whether HBRA areas exhibit higher cancer incidence.[90] The Kerala region is also the state of highest literacy and life expectancy in India. (Make of that what you will).

ARE ALL DOSES CUMULATIVE?

Intuitively, we are drawn to the view that low dose rates progressively received are proportionately less harmful

---

[90]http://www.thehindu.com/sci-tech/No-major-birth-defects-found-in-high-level-natural-radiation-areas-of-Kerala/article12543736.ece   July 2017

than high dose rates received quickly. This is a known phenomenon with toxins. At low doses warfarin, for example is a beneficial anticoagulant, but is toxic in higher amounts and is a popular rat poison. A patient, however, can tolerate warfarin over extended periods that would be fatal as a single dose, if the dose rates are controlled, a strategy occasionally used in murder mysteries involving poisons.

DOES DOSE RATE MATTER?

Closely allied to considerations of cumulative dose effects is the issue of dose rate. Much of the data for cancer risk is based on rapid exposures. There have been estimates that the effective dose can be reduced by a factor of up to three when the dose rate is low, as happens with chronic doses.[91] The ICRP recommends a Dose and Dose Rate Effectiveness Factor (RRDEF) of two. The consequences of this are that we can safely reduce the attributable lifetime cancer risk by a factor of two. To return to our earlier wine cellar analogy, a large amount of wine consumed in a few days is much more harmful than the same amount consumed over a year. There is a recorded instance of a man drinking a 750 mL bottle of whiskey in five minutes to win a bet[92]. This is surely an unwisely high dose rate.

HORMESIS – THE ULTIMATE HERESY?

There is a school of thought that proposes that very low levels of ionising radiation may be beneficial – an effect called 'radiation hormesis', a known phenomenon in other

---

[91] BEIR VII p 246-248.

[92] See http://www.news.com.au/lifestyle/health/man-dies-drinking-750ml-bottle-of-whiskey-in-five-minutes-to-win-bet/news-story/f712ee4f8bdaa03f557d8b4a83697671

fields of epidemiology as an adaptive response. Feinendegen, a prominent proponent of this hypothesis, concluded that the effect occurs because much of the damage to DNA comes from different sources at background radiation levels.[93] Furthermore, he asserts that low levels of ionising radiation offer a degree of adaptive response that prevents non-radiation damage and far outweighs any damage from radiation doses as a form of 'inoculation'. At higher doses, the radiation-induced damage becomes greater than the benefit provided by the adaptive response and the linear relationship is established. This is shown diagrammatically in Figure 7.5.

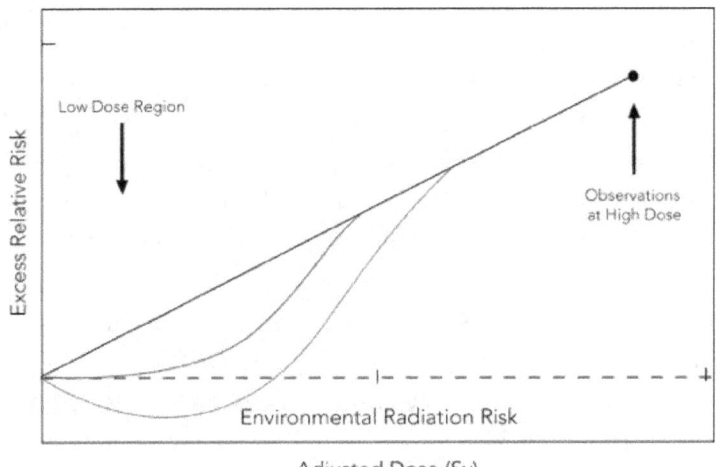

Figure 7.5: *Schematic view of the possible effects of small radiation doses on cancer risk.*
Top: *Linear no threshold*
Centre: *Linear-quadratic*
Lower: *Hormesis*

---

[93]LE Feinendegen. Evidence for beneficial low level radiation effects and radiation hormesis. Br J Radiol 2005;78:3–7.

Scott et al also support the hormesis concept, citing work on radiation response of laboratory rats to low levels of ionising radiation in support of the possible beneficial effects of CT scans.[94] Other work by Mitchel provides further support for the hormesis concept.[95],[96] This hormesis hypothesis has been supported in some studies by the evidence of workers in the nuclear industry having lower cancer incidence than the general population.[97]

This may to some extent be due to the higher general health level of staff recruited in the nuclear industry. There have also been suggestions that people living in houses with greater levels of radon gas show decreased incidence of lung cancer, but this is more anecdotal than scientific.

Others have debunked hormesis and quoted confounding factors such as the healthy worker effect (HWE) that proposes that nuclear workers are probably specially selected using rigorous pre-employment medicals, and are therefore an unrepresentative sample of the health of the general population.[98]

Nonetheless, hormesis is not yet proven or disproved, and there are precedents in toxicology. Human beings depend on clean water for survival, but pure water can itself be

---

[94] Bobby R Scott, Charles L Saunders, Ron E J Mitchell and Douglas R Boreham, CT Scans May Reduce Rather than Increase the Risk of Cancer, Journal of American Physicians and Surgeons, Vol 13, No 1, Spring 2008, 8-11

[95] R. E. J. Mitchel Low Doses of Radiation Reduce Risk in vivo. Dose-Response, 5(1) 1-10, 2007

[96] For further references on non-linear dose responses in toxicology, see also http://www.dose-response.com/ 19th June 2017

[97] https://www.ncbi.nlm.nih.gov/pubmed/20383052 November 2017

[98] http://www.gfstrahlenschutz.de/docs/hormeng2.pdf 16 Jun 2017

toxic, as we have evolved to depend on the traces of impurities that contribute to our electrolytes. As travellers to exotic places have found, however, excessive levels of water impurities can be fatal or can at least cause severe illness.

BEIR VII devotes an appendix to the hormesis concept, but leaves an open finding by concluding that any 'stimulatory' benefits that exceed any potential detrimental benefits cannot be assumed.[99]

If hormesis (or at least a lower threshold below which there is no effect) can be established, it would be a great benefit to society. Psychologically, a proven lack of effect would allay the alarm associated with low doses from environmental, industrial or medical uses of ionising radiation. Economically, it would allow radiation protection measures to reflect credible risks and may result in significant peace of mind as well as financial savings to the community. Contentious issues such as the clean-up following the British nuclear tests of the fifties and sixties in Australia could be addressed from a position of understanding rather than fear. In the future, it would make the storage of radioactive wastes much more manageable and address public concerns as nuclear energy ultimately takes its place in the energy jigsaw. The posturing by both sides of the nuclear debate could be transformed into a scientifically based rational approach to the risks involved.

In an interesting debate sponsored by the United Kingdom Radiological Council (UKRC) in 2005, two experts from each side attempted to reduce a complex problem to one

---
[99]BEIR VII, 335

simple principle after presentation of the opposing views.[100] The problem of extrapolating hard data based on higher doses (250 mSv) by a factor of a hundred to background dose levels was recognised. The proposition that 'there is no radiation risk to health at low doses' was defeated with 30% in favour, 54% against, and 16% undecided. This was not an overwhelming defeat for the radical hormesis proposition and while it is politically correct to adopt the LNT hypothesis, there are obviously still many unresolved issues in understanding very low dose rates.

Editorial, The British Journal of Radiology, 78 (2005), 1–2

★ ★ ★

Chapter 8:
Nuclear Accidents

I thought long and hard before including this section in this book as I have no qualifications or experience in nuclear technology, except 40 years using X-rays and isotopes in Nondestructive Testing (NDT). But friends who have asked about this project have posed a few questions and made a few comments worth sharing:

'It was terrible about all those deformed babies and animals in Russia after Chernobyl'
'I suppose that you're abandoning the book after Fukushima'
'Chernobyl killed millions'
'Won't they use nuclear power stations to make bombs?'
'Good on you – stick it up the greenies'
'Did you see Jane Fonda in *The China Syndrome*?'
'You're doing **WHAT**?'
'What if a nuclear power station goes off like a bomb'
...As well as miscellaneous remarks about Homer Simpson and his boss Mr Burns.

So here's a lay person's take on some nuclear accidents. My personal position is not uncritically nuclear, and things do go wrong in the best-regulated systems, so we should appreciate the risks of accidents and learn from them. As mentioned earlier, the first nuclear incident occurred about two billion years ago when a chain reaction was initiated in Gabon and ran out of control for a million years. Windscale, Three Mile Island, Chernobyl and Fukushima are examples of reactor malfunctions. These incidents have occurred in plant built in early years on nuclear energy. Nuclear technology has come a long way since then. In that time, we have moved from clunky adding machines for the few to iPads for the many, and from the original 1948 Holden to the modern motor car.

No nuclear power accident has involved a nuclear explosion. There have been explosions, but never nuclear explosions. The main hazard in nuclear reactors is losing control of the process and subsequent release of radioactive material.

Analysis of each accident has provided the basis for major improvement to the industry.

THE WINDSCALE FIRE (1957)

What Happened?

Windscale is located on the Cumbrian coast of Britain and had one of the original Magnox reactors used for producing plutonium for the British Atomic Weapons program.[101]

The Windscale and Calder Hall sites are now better known as Sellafield. The reactor over-heated and the graphite moderator caught fire. The fuel rods also ignited, sending the

---

[101] In one of the worst kept secrets ever, Calder Hall site was announced to the public as a nuclear power station that would produce electricity 'so cheaply it would be unnecessary to meter consumers'. See https://www.theguardian.com/uk/2003/mar/21/nuclear.world September 2017.

uranium, radioactive fission products including polonium and plutonium up in smoke. The health risk was caused by the radioactive iodine 131, which is readily absorbed by the body and concentrates in the thyroid gland. The isotope is also very efficiently channelled through milk, and milk produced in the reactor vicinity was immediately dumped. This was probably unnecessary, as the short half-life of I131 (eight days) meant that a few months' storage as cheese or powdered milk would have reduced the radioactivity to a negligible level. Windscale was the worst nuclear accident in Great Britain.

Probably the main root cause of the problem was the haste and crude design with which the British radioactive program was implemented during the early days of the Cold War. This design of reactor is no longer in operation.

THREE MILE ISLAND

What Happened?

The accident occurred in the TMI-2 reactor on 29th March 1979. One of the plant's main feed water pumps in the secondary (non-radioactive) cooling system failed. (See Reactor Coolant Pump in Figure 8.1) The exact cause of the pump failure was never determined; what is important is that the situation could have been prevented at many points along the way.

The result of the pump failure was that no heat was removed from the reactor. The reactor and turbine immediately shut down, but the extra heat made more steam in the primary (nuclear) water system, raising the pressure. A relief valve opened and remained open due to a design error, causing water to be released, resulting in further overheating

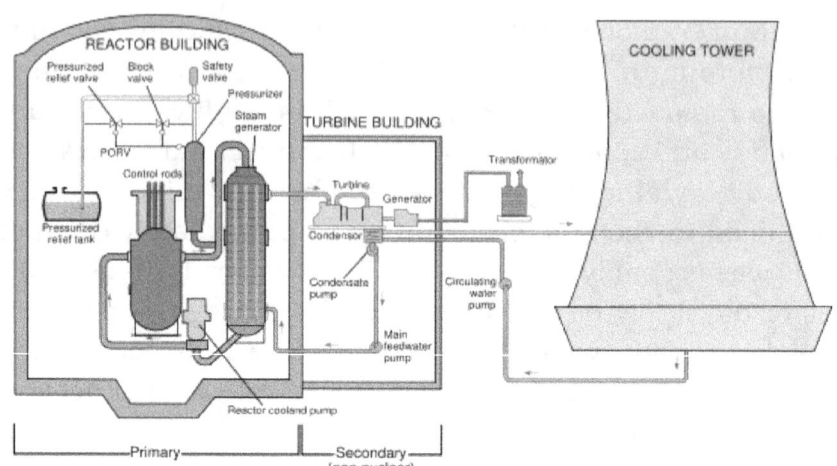

Figure 8.1: *Three Mile Island TMI-2*

of the core. There was no instrument to show the water level in the core, and so the incident was not recognised for what it was. Elsewhere, after a routine test two days earlier, other valves had been left closed instead of open, and this was not discovered until eight minutes into the accident. Large bubbles of steam in the reactor prevented cooling, causing false readings, which made the operators think the core was operating normally when it was not.

Initial indications that the relief valve was stuck open were ignored by the operators. This caused a rupture and leakage of primary (radioactive) water. After two hours, the top of the reactor core was exposed, damaging the fuel rods and releasing radioactive coolant, and generating hydrogen, which is thought to have exploded. The plant became seriously contaminated, half of the core was damaged, and much of the steam and hydrogen was controversially vented to the atmosphere, releasing 13 million Curies (480 peta-becquerels) of radioactive gases, but little of the more hazardous Iodine 131. The reactor vessel retained its integrity and contained the damaged fuel.

IN RETROSPECT

The initial cause seems to have been the mechanical failure of the coolant pump, but the disaster should have been avoided. The malfunction of the relief valve was a design error, as was the lack of an indication of the water level in the core. There was human error in leaving valves open that should have been closed, as well as in ignoring warnings that the relief valve was open. There is some controversy as to the wisdom in venting radioactivity to the atmosphere.

No fatalities or injuries were caused by the incident. The high amounts of naturally occurring radioactive radon gas probably masked any measurable radiation effects from the accident. The subsequent clean-up took 14 years at a cost of nearly one billion dollars (US), and the blow to the credibility of nuclear power was catastrophic. There were 51 orders for new reactors cancelled as a result. The reactor had operated for only three months and the accident occurred 12 days after the cinema release of *The China Syndrome*. The adjacent TMI-1 reactor of identical design is still functioning 38 years later.

There were mechanical failures, but the human factors were of most concern. Modern emergency procedures are based more on reacting to the situation than trying to over-analyse its cause. There were also many problems related to operating procedures and common-sense matters such as the ability to have line of sight to important controls. The identification and resolution of these issues have greatly contributed to the safety of modern nuclear power.

CHERNOBYL

There is no doubt that Chernobyl has been the most serious nuclear incident ever. On 26th April 1986, large amounts of short- and long-lived radionuclides were accidentally released to the atmosphere. Not only was the plant of outdated design but the political imperatives of the USSR in its dying stages made a bad situation much worse.

What Happened?[102]

Where does one start?

The Chernobyl number 4 reactor was one of four RBMK reactors. The RBMK (reactor high-power boiling water) was a water-cooled power reactor based on Russian graphite-moderated plutonium production military reactors.

The unit was undergoing a test to see whether the momentum of the turbines was sufficient for certain emergency electricity generation requirements. The planning for the test had taken months. As the experiment started, a regional power station went off-line unexpectedly, the reactor was required to maintain output and the test was postponed. So far so good.

The specially trained test team left the site. A skeleton crew more accustomed to coal fired generation with little nuclear experience was instructed to carry out the critical test on night shift. The stand-in operators were unaware of the protocol, and reduced power too quickly. This resulted in excessive production of xenon 135 (a 'nuclear poison'), which slowed down power generation to a fraction of the

---

[102]For a detailed account of the Chernobyl accident see Zhores A. Medvedev, *The Legacy of Chernobyl*, (Basil Blackwell, Oxford: 1990)

desired output.[103] To restore power, the inexperienced operators tried to increase the output by withdrawing the control rods further than allowed by regulations.

The extra output was still insufficient, but the experiment continued and the water flow was increased as part of the experiment. This water slowed the reaction more, and the rods were withdrawn further, resulting in a precarious situation – and no-one was aware just how precarious. When the reaction slows there is a decay of I135 to produce xenon 135 (Xe135) in the fuel rods. Reactors rely on the balance between Xe135 and I135. The process continued and the excess 'nuclear poison' was neutralised, causing a runaway reaction. The operators initiated a shutdown (SCRAM), inserting all the control rods.[104] Ironically, slow insertion accelerated the reaction. Fuel rods started to fracture, blocking the control rod columns – jamming the reactor at ten times its normal output.

Fuel rods melted, and steam pressure rose and caused an explosion, which ultimately blew a hole in the containment roof. The inrush of oxygen initiated a graphite fire that contributed to the spread of radioactive contamination to outlying areas with radioactive Cs137, I131, Sr90 and other radionuclides. There was only one radiation measuring instrument on the site and that was 'buried somewhere' as 'the accident was not in the plan'.[105]

---

[103]When Xenon 135 builds up in the fuel rods, it absorbs neutrons and therefore slows down the nuclear reaction.

[104]'SCRAM' stands for 'safety control rod axe man', a phrase supposedly coined by Enrico Fermi at the world's first nuclear reactor, where a man was positioned above the reactor to cut the rope holding the control rods into the reactor and stop the process in the event of an emergency.

[105]Medvedev, *Legacy of Chernobyl*, 52

The fire fighters were completely unaware of the radioactive hazard they faced. Their heroic attempts resulted in their immediate deaths from acute radiation exposure, receiving up to 15 Sv (15,000 mSv). A radioactive cloud covered much of Europe for years afterwards.

There were design flaws in the way that the reactor dealt with steam formation in the coolant water. Steam is not an effective moderator, and this contributed to the runaway reaction. There were also faults in the design of the control rods and water channels. The design did not account for distortion due to overheating, which prevented re-insertion of the control rods. The containment vessel was ineffective, and allowed escape of contaminants.

If the design issues were not serious enough, the operators were inexperienced, violated procedures and were unfamiliar with the plant in their charge. There was an element of desperation in carrying out the tests on the reactor, as there would not have been another time window for carrying out the trials for twelve months. The situation was compared to an inexperienced 747 crew conducting critical experiments on the engines during a fully booked commercial flight. It was an almost inevitable accident in a doomed environment, for which surely management must bear the greatest responsibility for deficiencies in design and operation.

CONSEQUENCES

Chernobyl was one of the great preventable disasters caused by humans of all time. The original reactor remains encased in a concrete sarcophagus. By 1991 the three other reactors at the Chernobyl site were decommissioned. Acute radiation sickness affected 234 people, of whom 28 died within three months. There were 15 subsequent deaths soon after, and the remainder survived to live with the consequences of their heroism. These figures are approximate as accounts vary.

The estimation of the likely cancer burden from airborne radioactivity to the population of Europe is a complex statistical and demographic study, but applying modern methodology, Cardis and co-workers predicted that by 2065, about 16,000 cases of thyroid cancer and 25,000 cases of other cancers may be caused by the incident.[106]

It is unlikely that Chernobyl will result in any discernible increase in overall cancer rates to the general population, except for thyroid cancer in children. The thyroid gland in the front of the neck concentrates iodine from the diet and blood. Radioactive I135 concentrating in the thyroid can cause cancers in thyroid cells. Children in Gomel Oblast in neighbouring Belarus received the worst dose of around 750 mSv. Of the 18 million children exposed to radioactive iodine (I135) from Chernobyl, there were 6,000 cases of thyroid cancer.[107]

Fortunately, most of those cancers were successfully treated with I135, the same isotope that had caused the cancer. The estimated longer-term radioactive caesium dose to Gomel Oblast was 10mSv – similar to an abdominal CT scan[108]. The effects of caesium 137 (a gamma emitter) are much longer term due to its longer half-life (30 years) than I135 (eight days).

---

[106]Elizabeth Cardis et al, Estimates of the cancer burden in Europe from the Chernobyl Accident, Int J Cancer, 119 (2006)

[107]http://www.unscear.org/unscear/en/chernobyl.html 16 June 2017

[108]Drozdovitch et al, Radiation exposure to the population of Europe following the Chernobyl accident, Radiat Prot Dosimetry, 2007; 123(4), 515

Much has been made of Chernobyl's genetic legacy of Down's syndrome, congenital abnormalities, miscarriages and perinatal mortality. The 2001 UNSCEAR report concludes that there is no unambiguous evidence for an increase in birth defects attributable to Chernobyl in either Ukraine or Belarus.[109] You might say they dodged a bullet. It could have been much worse.

FUKUSHIMA

I started researching this book in 2007 and was well advanced (or so I thought) when the Fukushima catastrophe occurred; some of my friends assumed that I would abandon the project. Exactly the reverse has occurred as the power station withstood ten times its design earthquake load, there were no acute cases of radiation sickness, and very unlikely to be any measurable long term stochastic effects, despite dire predictions.[110] The death of 16,000 people and dislocation from the tsunami seems sometimes overlooked in the rush to ring the alarm bells over nuclear energy. The nuclear legacy was dislocation from the evacuation of towns around the site.

On 11th March 2011 a severe earthquake off the coast of Japan rocked the east coast north of Tokyo. The resulting tsunami sent a ten-metre wall of water across the coast, demolishing nearly everything in its path and ultimately taking the lives of 16,000 people, with a further 3,000 unaccounted for. Although there were no deaths linked to ionising radiation, the social cost was terrible as people's

---

[109]UNSCEAR 2000: Report of the United Nations Scientific Committee on the Effects of Atomic Radiation to the General Assembly (2000)

[110]Richard Broinowski, Fallout from Fukishima, Scribe, 2012

lives were completely disrupted by evacuation, stress and loss of community.[111]

The flow-on effect was dislocation of communities. In the path of this tsunami were four nuclear power plants, with a total of 14 nuclear reactors. The most severely affected was the Fukushima Daiichi (no 1) plant, when the failure of water cooling pumps caused by the earthquake and tsunami halted the supply of cooling water to reactors 1, 2 and 3. This immediately caused overheating in the reactor cores of all three. This plant was designed to withstand an earthquake of force 8 on the Richter scale, but the earthquake in this case was a force 9 i.e. ten times the design earthquake force, and the plant still survived. The added effects of the tsunami caused a complete loss of power to the pumps when they were flooded and cooling was lost.

In May 2013, 80 international scientists analysed the available information on Fukushima and released a communiqué of their present view of the Fukushima Nuclear Accident under the auspices of the United Nations Scientific Committee on the Effects of Atomic Radiation (UNSCEAR) with the following comments:

On the whole, the exposure of the Japanese population was low, or very low, leading to correspondingly low risks of health effects later in life. The actions taken to protect the public (evacuation and sheltering) significantly reduced the radiation exposures that would have otherwise been received, concluded the Committee 'These measures reduced the potential exposure by up to a factor of 10. If that had not been the case, we might have seen the

---

[111] For an account of the consequences of Fukushima see: Broinowski, Richard. 2012 *Fallout from Fukushima*. Melbourne:Scribe.

cancer rates rising and other health problems emerging over the next several decades,' said Wolfgang Weiss, Chair, UNSCEAR report on radiological Impact of the Fukushima-Daiichi accident.

The doses delivered for the two most significant radionuclides were quite different: doses to the thyroid mainly from iodine-131 ranged up to several tens of milligray [equivalent to milliSieverts] and were received within a few weeks after the accident; the whole-body (or effective) doses mainly from caesium-134 and caesium-137 ranged up to ten or so milliSieverts (mSv) and will be received over the lifetime of those exposed. The additional exposures received by most Japanese people in the first year and subsequent years due to the radioactive releases from the accident are less than the doses received from natural background radiation (which is about 2.1 mSv per year). This is particularly the case for Japanese people living away from Fukushima, where annual doses of around 0.2 mSv from the accident are estimated, arising primarily through ingestion of radionuclides in food.

No radiation-related deaths or acute effects have been observed among nearly 25,000 workers (including TEPCO employees and contractors) involved at the accident site.

Given the small number of highly exposed workers, it is unlikely that excess cases of thyroid cancer due to radiation exposure would be detectable. Special health examinations will be given to workers with exposures above 100 mSv including annual monitoring of the thyroid, stomach, large intestine and lung for cancer as a means to monitor for potential late radiation-related health effects at the individual level.[112]

---

[112] http://www.unis.unvienna.org/unis/en/pressrels/2013/unisinf475.html 25th July 2013

None of this considers the distress, alienation and loss of family caused by these events, which were triggered by a natural disaster that nobody could have predicted. It is likely that the burden of nuclear disasters will ultimately be greater on people's mental well-being than on their physical health.

NON-NUCLEAR DISASTERS OF THE TWENTIETH CENTURY

Chernobyl was one of the most important manufactured disasters that has ever occurred, but was by no means the most catastrophic in terms of lives lost. The immediate death toll seems less dramatic in comparison to some other disasters of human origin:

> The failure of Banqiao Dam at Henan, China in 1975 killed an estimated 26,000 people immediately and another 145,000 died during subsequent epidemics and famine.
>
> The Bhopal disaster in India, 1984, was estimated to have had a death toll of nearly 3,000 people initially. At least another 15,000 subsequently died from related illnesses.
>
> The Great Smog of London, in 1952, was calculated by medical services to have killed 4,000 people initially, and another 8,000 died in the weeks and months that followed. The smog was due to particle and gas emissions from coal fires combined with exceptional weather.
>
> Despite these statistics, we continue with the construction of dams for water storage and hydro electricity for our daily needs as well as chemical plants and the

> combustion of coal for energy. None of this is to justify the most terrible things that happened at Chernobyl and what might have happened at Fukushima, but it is useful to view events in proportion.

However, nuclear energy is such a sensitive issue that Chernobyl derailed what had been an ambitious nuclear power program and formed a fledgling environmental movement into a potent political force in Russia. As well, the events became a rallying point for achieving Ukrainian and Belarusian independence in 1991.

There has been a major overhaul in both essential design and operating parameters of nuclear reactors that has learnt much from former incidents, just as shipping is safer because of the lessons learnt from the Titanic and air traffic control has been enhanced following the tragic collision at Tenerife which killed 583 in 1977.

RATING NUCLEAR EVENTS

Nuclear events have been classified by international agreement according to their severity – the lowest being minor events with no off-site consequences, right up to those that have widespread health and environmental effects outside the site.[113]

- Level 1 **Anomalies** such as breach of procedures
- Level 2 **Incidents** which are more serious than a level 1 anomaly, and may result in an individual

---

[113]Based on the International Nuclear Event Scale – see https://www.iaea.org/sites/default/files/ines.pdf 12 June 2017

worker exceeding permissible dose limits. The event at Forsmark NPP (Sweden) in 2006 was classified as Level 2, although this classification is still disputed by a former employee. Sweden agreed at referendum in 1980 to phase out nuclear power by 2010 and will become an importer of electricity.
- Level 3 **Serious incidents** where groups of workers may receive doses up to one mSv, with spread of radioactivity into secondary circuits – indicative of a breakdown of safety systems, but no off site risk. Such an event occurred at the Vandellos (Spain) in 1989 and the THORP plant at Sellafield (UK) in 2005.
- Level 4 **Accidents** with no offsite risk, where groups of workers receive up to 10mSv, the facility experiences damage, or a worker receives a dose that may result in severe acute effects. Such an event occurred at Saint-Laurent NPP (France) in 1980 due to partial damage of the reactor core.
- Level 5 **Accidents with offsite risk** where there is a release of radioactive materials, and the facility sustains severe damage. Such events occurred at Windscale reactor (UK) in 1957 with release of radioactivity, and at Three Mile Island in 1979 due to damage to the reactor.
- Level 6 **Serious accidents**, where a major release of radioactivity occurs, necessitating full implementation of countermeasures and local emergency plans. Such an event occurred at Kyshtym Reprocessing Plant (USSR) in 1957 based on the release of radioactivity.
- Level 7 **Major accidents** where there is a large fraction of the radioactive material at the facility released sufficient to cause acute health effects over a wide area

and long term environmental consequences. Chernobyl (1986) and Fukushima (2011) are the only examples of a major accident. The non-nuclear equivalent of a Level 7 event would be the Bhopal disaster in India in 1984.

THE HUMAN FACTOR

One common thread through the brief sample of the major nuclear incidents is the fallibility of human beings, particularly for technologies in their early stages. That fallibility has seen disasters in flight, rail and road transport, and a multitude of chemical and process industries. The same fallible human beings also build and operate aeroplanes, chemical plants, railways, fossil fuel and hydroelectric plants. Other fallible human beings are destined to fall from buildings while installing solar panels and towers while installing wind turbines.

★ ★ ★

Chapter 9:
Nuclear Politics

The first discovery of uranium in Australia was near Carcoar in 1894. Before World War II very few Australians had any interest or understanding of nuclear issues, even though Australians Lawrence and William Bragg and Marcus Oliphant had played significant roles in unravelling the mysteries of the atom. We mined uranium, but mainly to obtain the associated radium as Ra226 for its supposed therapeutic properties.

THE HUNTERS HILL SMELTER

A century ago, the early exploitation of uranium ores for therapeutic radium left us with an environmental legacy. From 1911 to 1915 a smelter was established in Hunters Hill to receive and process 2,000 tons of uranium ore concentrate to extract 2 grams of radium. All the decay products of the concentrate (1% uranium oxide) were present in the tailings, which were dumped on the site. The Hunters Hill region has since become highly desirable harbour-side real estate, but the question of residual tailings is now causing alarm to residents. A parliamentary enquiry was undertaken in 2008 to consider the implications of remediation efforts undertaken in the 1960s. Certain parts of the suspect site were found to have radiation levels several times background levels.

World War II changed everything. America developed and deployed two atomic bombs in Japan. By 1942 the Australian government had taken control of uranium, but interest was subdued until 1945.[114] After the Japanese atomic bombs it did not take a giant leap of the imagination for the post war British Government to imagine nuclear weapons in the hands of potential enemies as the Cold War deepened. A few nuclear weapons strategically delivered could bring the United Kingdom to its knees. This no doubt focused the minds of the British, who had just weathered the Blitz and then returned the favour over German cities such as Dresden in the closing stages of the war.

Britain had shared her nuclear technology with American allies during wartime, but there was no such American reciprocity in the post war years. British security was suspect (as evidenced by a series of spy scandals) and the United States was entering a more secretive phase with the McMahon Act, which made it illegal to share nuclear technology. Britain urgently needed to develop a nuclear weapons capability to form part of its defences in the new Cold War environment. Britain was rich in intellectual capacity and had laboratories that had survived World War II.

But a nuclear program is about more than just building bombs. Delivery systems need to be tested; would weapons be delivered by bomber or remotely by rockets? All of this needs vast tracts of unoccupied territory for rocket tests, nuclear test sites and featureless terrain for long distance

---

[114]Alice Cawte, Atomic Australia, (Sydney, NSW University Press:1992) 3-6

air navigational experience if delivery was to be by aircraft. So, it seemed to Britain that this was a good time to resuscitate the notion of the Empire. They had nuclear technology but no territory in which to prove it. The Empire as a unifying concept in Australia had taken a backward step after the fall of Singapore, with wartime disagreements and Curtin's famous 'turn to America' policy. This made the United States our dominant ally in the latter stages of World War II.

Canada was Britain's partner of choice, but that dominion was now within the American sphere of influence, strategically located between Eastern Russia and continental United States. The Berlin airlift of 1948 brought America and Britain together briefly in shared adversity, during which Australia was temporarily frozen out of any plans of uranium for technology exchange. Britain subsequently returned to discuss atomic tests with Australia. America's distrust of British security extended to denial of British access to their test facility Eniwetak in the Pacific.

Evidence suggests that the notion to carry out nuclear testing in Australia predated the Menzies era, and was the policy of the Chifley government as part of a three-pronged approach to restructure industry, higher education and defence.[115] In 1949 Chifley was replaced as Prime Minister by Menzies, also keen to invigorate the post war economy with the assistance of atomic energy. The position of Canada in the American sphere left only South Africa and New Zealand as other possible sites for the British nuclear program. This gave Menzies the opportunity to revive the arrangements previously initiated by Chifley.

---

[115]Reynolds Australia's Bid for the Atomic Bomb, (Melbourne, MUP: 2000) , 37,38

By 1950, the Soviet Union had atomic weapons, there was war on the Korean peninsula, China had been taken over by the Communists and there was unrest in Malaya and Indo China. The so-called (now discredited) 'Domino Theory' was bringing the perception of a communist threat to Australia's doorstep. Federal government negotiations were complicated by the states' rights claims of Sir Thomas Playford of South Australia. Playford was determined to maximise the benefit of a major asset in a state otherwise starved of natural resources. Uranium seemed the best card he had.[116]

In return for assisting the British with their nuclear tests, Australia would receive access to British technology and training for Australian engineers and scientists as part of post war reconstruction. The tangible demonstration of this was a research reactor at Lucas Heights NSW – a down payment of the British contribution to an Australian nuclear program. This would assist Australia's entry to the nuclear club and the ability to fight above her weight internationally. Nuclear engineering became a study within the University of Technology (later the University of New South Wales), under the Vice Chancellorship of Professor JP Baxter, a pioneer in development of uranium enrichment formerly from Tube Alloys[117]. The Australian Atomic Energy Commission (AAEC) was established in 1953 with bipartisan support and it was no coincidence that Baxter also became head of the AAEC which operated the new Hi Flux Atomic Reactor (HIFAR). Other roles for the AAEC

---

[116]Cawte, Atomic Australia, 36

[117]'Tube Alloys' was the wartime British name for their atomic energy project. Baxter had pioneered the gasification of Uranium for enrichment while at Tube Alloys.

included training engineers in nuclear power and research. HIFAR was originally to be located at Maroubra – close to Baxter's University of Technology, but was built at Lucas Heights. This probably explained Baxter's decision to live in a more modest suburb of Sydney, midway between these two institutions, while his fellow professors populated the North Shore and Eastern Suburbs.

Those with an enquiring turn of mind might also see connections between the atomic energy program, the Australian National University (ANU) in Canberra and the Snowy Mountains Hydroelectric Authority (SMHEA). The ANU was to be a research centre of nuclear knowledge headed by an eminent nuclear scientist Sir Marcus Oliphant (who had played a part in starting the Manhattan Project). The nearby SMHEA had similarities to the Tennessee Valley Authority (whose electricity had powered the uranium enrichment program for the Manhattan Project) and the Hartford Hydro scheme in Washington State that had powered the plutonium enrichment. The SMHEA was the great nation building project of the post war era, attracting skilled immigrants to build a major infrastructure project that developed skills in engineering and was located strategically away from the coast. Major generating units were located well below ground for security. The professed aims of the Snowy were diversion of water inland and domestic power generation.

The British nuclear tests did go ahead, and successfully demonstrated that British nuclear weapons had caught up with the Americans by 1957, to the extent that the United States eventually agreed to a sharing of technology with Britain, as well as the Nevada desert test sites. This made further Australian contribution of little value. The so-called

'Fourth British Empire,' forged in post war adversity lasted only a few years and collapsed with a whimper in the mid 1960s as Australia once again turned to America as the British turned to Europe. To put Australia's role in global atomic testing in perspective, the British tests in Australia comprised 1.72% of the total yield of all nuclear tests up to 1993.[118]

There has been much debate about the effects of the British atomic tests on Australian military personnel. A report was commissioned by the Federal government in 2006. This report concluded that there was a significant increase in the likelihood of both developing and dying from cancer among those working on the tests.[119] The report concluded that there was no evidence that the excess cancers and cancer deaths were caused by radiation exposure at the test sites. A contributing factor was the high smoking prevalence relative to the Australian population with whom rates were compared. Asbestos was also a likely contributor to cancers in naval personnel, who were overrepresented in cancer statistics, despite air force personnel having flown through the atomic dust that followed detonation.

The withdrawal of the British in the 1960s left nuclear and political fallout that still bedevils us today. There were two attempts to secure weapons.[120] The first was through

---

[118]https://en.wikipedia.org/wiki/List_of_nuclear_weapons_tests 6 July 2017.

[119]Richard Gun, Jacqueline Parsons, Philip Ryan, Philip Crouch and Janet Hiller, Australian participants in British nuclear tests in Australia, Vol 2: Mortality and cancer incidence May 2006

[120]Jim Walsh, Surprise Down Under, 1-14

procurement (1956–1963) in the later years of the Menzies era. A second attempt was through developing a local capability after 1964 – initiated by Menzies, and enthusiastically adopted by John Gorton until stopped by the incoming Whitlam government, which ratified the NPT in 1973. The legacy of the tests became increasingly politically sensitive with higher levels of tertiary education raising political awareness (another Menzies legacy to the baby boomer generation), environmental awareness, sensitivity to indigenous rights and emerging nationalism. In later decades Labor governments were elected with no prior association with or political baggage from the decisions made in the fifties and sixties.

Subsequently the British and Australian recollections of events began to diverge, especially after the report of the McClelland Royal Commission of 1984.[121], [122] The British government contributed $45 million to the cost of site rehabilitation and $13 million in reparations to Indigenous people affected by the tests. But even the clean-up operation of the 1990s was subject to allegations of shoddy and unprofessional work. If such allegations are true, we have much to learn about managing nuclear weapons waste as all but 900 grams of the original 24 kg of plutonium plus seven tonnes of depleted uranium of the British tests remain unaccounted for.[123]

---

[121]Commonwealth of Australia, The Report of the Royal Commission into British Nuclear Tests in Australia: Conclusions and Recommendations, (RCBNTA) AGPS, Canberra, 1985.

[122]Dieter Michel, Villains, Victims and Heroes: Contested Memory and the British Nuclear Tests in Australia, Journal of Australian Studies, Issue 80?, January 2004, 221-228.

[123]Alan Parkinson, Maralinga: Australia's Nuclear Waste Cover-up, (Sydney, ABC:2007), 7

With the British withdrawal, what would be the role of the AAEC? The AAEC was ultimately rebadged in 1987 as the Australian Nuclear Science and Technology Organisation (ANSTO). The new body was to abandon any interests in nuclear energy. There were by then eight universities involved in relevant studies and thirty-one students working on AAEC-sponsored research.[124] The higher education and industrial infrastructure were in place for a nuclear program, but the withdrawal of British interest in Australia left us with no immediate nuclear future, but a large investment in nuclear energy including the research reactor. In 1969 a short-lived plan was in place for a nuclear power station on federal land at Jervis Bay in NSW. It was to be owned by the Commonwealth, and operated by the Electricity Commission of NSW. Other states also toyed with the idea of nuclear power, but in a country blessed with cheap steaming coal and with no climate change awareness, the nuclear option was seen as too expensive. Australia's attempt at entry into the nuclear club was probably one of the last of Prime Minister John Gorton's pronouncements. By March 1971 he was replaced by William McMahon and the initiative was squashed by Treasury and abandoned by 1972. The cost to Australia of this nuclear adventure was $172 million for negligible tangible result.

The AAEC then turned its attention to enrichment, with the objective of exporting enriched uranium, a much higher value export than basic yellowcake. Despite some technical success by the early 1980s, the plan was later abandoned. Since then the main Commonwealth sponsored nuclear

---
[124]Reynolds Australia's Bid, 142

developments have been the National Medical Cyclotron at Camperdown (used in PET Scans), continued development of Synroc for waste storage and OPAL, and the new research reactor at Lucas Heights.

The AAEC had been responsible for mining uranium at Rum Jungle in the 1950s, and constructed the Ranger Mine during the period of the Whitlam government. Under the subsequent Coalition government the venture was sold back to private enterprise. From 1975 to 1977 there was a major review of nuclear power and uranium under Mr Justice Fox, looking at both mining and nuclear power, as well as its environmental impact on a sensitive region. The outcome of this review was that mining continued under strict controls of both the use of uranium and its environmental impact.

MARY KATHLEEN

The Mary Kathleen project is an interesting indicator of Australia's nuclear history. In 1956, as all the pieces of the nuclear jigsaw were falling into place, an agreement was reached between the AAEC and the UK Atomic Energy Authority (UKAEA) for technology exchange and the establishment of Mary Kathleen Uranium (MKU). Following the discovery of the ore body in 1954, a syndicate was established to exploit the deposit. This syndicate ultimately extended to include Rio Tinto (53%), Australian Oil Exploration (35%) and the original prospectors (9%). UKAEA contributed some of the venture capital to fast track the project and entered a contract to purchase 4,082 tons of yellowcake for $80 million in 1956. The first uranium was delivered in 1958. In 1963, when the contract was completed, the site was mothballed pending further contracts. By this time,

MKU's share register comprised Conzinc Rio Tinto (51%), Kathleen Investments (35%) and the public (14%).

By 1974, as part of Rex Connor's plan for taking control of Australia's resources, the Australian government, through AAEC, obtained 42% of the shares of MKU, with Conzinc Rio Tinto retaining 51% and the public shareholding dropping to 7%. A second contract had been negotiated for uranium by this time and the mine operated until 1983 when oversupply had made it uneconomical.

Research continued into enrichment until 1976 in the hope that Australia would be a vertically integrated player in the uranium supply chain, but that expertise has now dissipated. The Hawke Government adopted a controversial 'Three Mines' policy in 1984 to restrict any further uranium mining, but with the closure of the Narbalek mine in the Northern Territory this became a 'Two Mines' policy. There was a political imperative for the Hawke government to accommodate the Roxby Downs mine in South Australia, one of the original three mines, to maintain support for the ALP in the upcoming State election.

LATER NUCLEAR POWER REVIEWS

The Howard Coalition government commissioned the UMPNER study into nuclear options as pressure mounted to reduce carbon emissions from fossil fired power stations.[125] The recommendations of their 2006 report included:
- Australia can significantly increase uranium exports, but local enrichment is unlikely to be viable.

---

[125]Commonwealth of Australia, Uranium Mining, Processing and Nuclear Energy – Report to the Prime Minister by the Uranium Mining, Processing and Nuclear Energy Task Force, December 2006.

- While legacy issues such as Chernobyl are acknowledged, nuclear technology for power production has advantages in both emissions and safety.
- Proliferation risks were associated with secret enrichment plants, not spent fuel from correctly managed reactors.
- Australia could build 25 reactors of 1,000 MW capacity by 2050 to supply 25 per cent of the projected national demand and reduce the growth of emissions by 17 per cent.

This report had an air of unrealistic optimism about it. Not surprisingly many Australians greeted these recommendations with some dismay, particularly as most of the possible reactor sites would need to be in prime coastal locations for access to cooling water. This set off a wave of panic among sitting Coastal MPs and has dropped off the radar.

★ ★ ★

Chapter 10:
Epilogue

*Please don't get me wrong: I'm not trying to be pro-nuclear.
I'm just pro-arithmetic.*

Professor David J C Mackay[126]

'Tell 'em what you told 'em'

This has been a long and at times difficult slog through the complex subject of ionising radiation. I hope the early semi-technical information did not put you off, but we need some understanding to make decisions based on science rather than phobias. Ionising radiation cannot be experienced by any of our five senses, but explaining with metaphors and analogies helps to understand what must seem like abstract concepts. Alpha and beta particles, as well as gamma rays and X-rays are 'similar but different' types of ionising radiation that we can measure. We use these ionising radiations in medicine, industry and even in the home to gain a benefit and improve our lives.

Nuclear weapons are the ugly face of radioactivity and somehow the world needs to establish a way to control their proliferation. The Korean peninsula looms as a major test of

---

[126]https://www.ted.com/talks/david_mackay_a_reality_check_on_renewables/transcript November 2017

the nuclear states to demonstrate their resolve. If our intuitive fear of the unknown can be overcome, nuclear power offers a way of low-carbon generation – even if only for the intervening decades until the holy grail of base load generation from renewables is a reality. Nuclear waste is an issue, but common sense in isolation and shielding can surely address that. No country is better situated than Australia to manage nuclear waste.

We cannot avoid radiation in our lives – especially when we take advantage of life saving nuclear diagnosis and treatment. But ionising radiation can kill us within days if delivered in extremely large doses to our whole body. At lesser doses it can make us very sick and might even kill us. At even lower doses, these direct acute effects are replaced by random effects and the possibility of cancer. Yet we treat cancers with massive doses of as much as 50 Sv to very concentrated areas of the body – often causing temporary sickness in the process. This gives us the paradox of using a large dose of radiation to cure what might have been caused by a small dose.

We worry too much about the safety of nuclear industry. It is estimated that there have been up to 200 people killed in non-military incidents by large radiation doses since the first fatality in America in 1945. The biggest peacetime event of acute fatal dose occurred in the Chernobyl disaster of 1986. Others have occurred due to lost radioactive materials, malpractice and more recently by political assassination. There were no fatal doses received at Three Mile Island, Fukushima or any other nuclear power station.

But we now have ways of calculating exposure risks using the conservative Linear no Threshold (LNT) model. In our lifetimes around forty per cent of us will contract cancer and half of those cases will be terminal. Some of these will occur naturally without any external agency and some will be triggered by environmental carcinogens. There are 120 proven carcinogens recognised by the World Health Organisation (WHO), of which one is ionising radiation. Some of the key metrics for ionising radiation are:

- We are now able to estimate that for a dose of 0.1 Sv (100 mSv) the lifetime extra risk of contracting cancer is around 1% and for dying from cancer is around 0.5%.
- For a dose of 10mSv the lifetime probability of contacting cancer is around 0.1% and for dying from cancer is around 0.05%, so a lumbar CT scan will raise your lifetime death from cancer risk from 20% to 20.05%. Not bad odds – but don't overdo the CT scans.
- These small changes in statistics that are highly variable can be difficult to measure.
- There are probably many more fatalities caused by stress from worrying about radiation than will ever be caused by the radiation itself.

There is some debate on whether these projections are over-estimated at low doses and there may even be a benefit in very low doses. Just as setting traffic speed limits will reduce the risk of road fatalities, but will never eliminate them, setting legal exposure limits will never guarantee a risk-free exposure, but will greatly reduce the threat.

Australia has the largest deposits of uranium in the world but has no participation in the nuclear industry beyond mining uranium ore and exporting uranium oxide. As coal fired power stations age and base-load replacement is needed until renewables can provide base load power there is a place at the table for nuclear power in the energy mix. If we can overcome our fear of radiation there is also an opportunity for Australia with its abundant resources and open spaces to become a major supplier of yellowcake (even enriched uranium) and be a repository for nuclear waste storage until renewables can supply base load power all day every day.

We are rapidly developing renewable energy at quite an impressive rate, and if there is convincing evidence that our base load needs can be served by renewables at a reasonable cost, then Australia will have no need to even consider nuclear or coal energy. The renewable contribution to our national energy is 17%, of which over half is hydro. There is little upside for hydro in a flat dry continent. With the greatest respect for renewable proponents, I cannot see the gap being filled by non-hydro renewable power growing from 8 per cent of our annual needs to 92 per cent in the foreseeable future.

It's time to stop shouting and start talking

Appendices

Appendix A
Periodic table of the elements

Appendix B
Natural decay sequence of U238

Step	Mother Isotope	Daughter Isotope	Decay Half Life	Radiation Emitted
1	Uranium 238	Thorium 234	4.47 Billion Years	α particle
2	Thorium 234	Protactinium 234	24.1 days	β particle
3	Protactinium 234	Uranium 234	6.7 hr	β particle
4	Uranium 234	Thorium 230	1.17 minutes	α particle
5	Thorium 230	Radium 226	75,000 years	α particle
6	Radium 226	Radon 222	1600 years	α particle
7	Radon 222	Polonium 218	3.8 days	α particle
8	Polonium 218	Lead 214	3 minutes	α particle
9	Lead 214	Bismuth 214	26.8 minutes	β particle
10	Bismuth 214	Polonium 214	19.7 minutes	β particle
11	Polonium 214	Lead 210	0.000164 secs	α particle
12	Lead 210	Bismuth 210	22.3 years	β particle
13	Bismuth 210	Polonium 210	5 days	β particle
14	Polonium 210	Lead 206	138 days	α particle*

*polonium 210 is the assassin's radioactive poison of choice

Appendix C
Large and small quantities

LARGE UNITS

Prefix	Name	Decimal	Index	Example
None	None	1	10^0	becquerel
Kilo (k)	Thousand	1,000	10^3	kilobecquerel
Mega (M)	Million	1,000,000	10^6	megabecquerel
Giga (G)	Billion	1,000,000,000	10^9	gigabecquerel
Tera (T)	Thousand billion	1,000,000,000,000	10^{12}	terabecquerel

SMALL UNITS

Prefix	Name	Decimal	Index	Example
None	None	1	10^0	Sievert
Milli (m)	Thousandth	0.001	10^{-3}	milliSievert
Micro (μ)	Millionth	0.000001	10^{-6}	microsievert
Nano (n)	Billionth	0.000000001	10^{-9}	nanosievert
Pico (p)	Thousand billionth	0.000000000001	10^{-12}	picosievert

EXAMPLES:

- If a one dollar coin is about two millimetres thick:
  - one mega dollar in $1 coins would make a pile two km high
  - one giga dollar would make a pile two thousand km high.
- A human hair is half a micron thick (5×10^{-5} metres – 0.05mm). This is equal to 50,000 nanometres.
- The first personal computers of the 1970s had a storage capacity of 75 kb (75,000 bytes) on a floppy disk.

- The first hard discs had a capacity around 10Mb (10million bytes)..
- Standard personal computers have a minimum storage capacity of 200 Gb (200 billion bytes)
- For a hundred dollars, you can buy a storage disk with a capacity of 1 Tb (one thousand giga bytes).
- Planck's Constant for calculating the energy of a photon of an Electromagnetic wave:

$$6.626176 \times 10^{-34} = 0.0000000000000000000000000000000006626176.$$

★ ★ ★

Appendix D
Exposure units - derivation of the sievert (Sv)

The unit of dose equivalent is the sievert (Sv), which was developed as follows:

IONISING POTENTIAL

Before the development of the SI units for radiation measurement, there was an arbitrary unit called the roentgen (R) as a measure of the ionising of EMR capacity in air. One roentgen is the amount of radiation that would produce a charge of 2.58×10^{-4} coulombs per kilogram of air (C/kg). There is no SI equivalent, as the old roentgen unit has limited use outside America, but you can use coulombs per kilogram (C/kg) if you must. It is a measure of radiation output in air and is not a measure of absorbed dose in humans. Absorbed dose is more important, as the interaction with human tissue is more important than the interaction with air. 'Roentgen' is still used for measuring the output of X-ray equipment

ABSORBED DOSE – THE BODY'S ABSORPTION

When a person is exposed to radiation, energy is deposited in the tissues of the body. The amount of energy deposited per unit of mass of human tissue is called the absorbed dose. Absorbed dose is measured using the Gray

(Gy). One Gy is equivalent to 104 ergs per gram of tissue. The old unit is the rad (radiation absorbed dose). One gray equals 100 rads.

DOSE EQUIVALENT – ALPHA BETA OR GAMMA?

Although we can define the amount of radiation and its ability to deposit energy in tissue (absorbed dose), we need one more factor to estimate what damage is done to humans by that energy. Research has shown that some radiation is much more damaging than others, with alpha particles being the most harmful – if they can reach a susceptible body organ. The alpha particle is a large positively charged particle with a very high capacity for interacting with negatively charged electrons and damaging covalent bonds. X-rays, β particles and gamma rays have less damaging capacity but are much more penetrating. To calculate the dose equivalent, we use the formula:

Dose equivalent = Absorbed dose x (quality factor)

Typical quality factors are shown below.

Radiation type	Factor
X-rays	1
Gamma Rays	1
Beta Rays	1
Neutrons and protons	10
Alpha particles	20

Radiation Quality factors

The **sievert** is the unit for measuring radiation damage potential to human beings.
- For gamma rays, X-rays and beta rays, one gray equals one sievert.
- For neutron and proton radiation, one gray equals 10 sieverts.
- For alpha particles one gray equals 20 sieverts.
- Diagnostic radiography doses are often recorded as grays, and are the same equivalent in sieverts.
- Mixed doses of radiation are bundled together as sieverts to give a measure of ionising damage capability.

For a comprehensive conversion chart see www.civildefensemuseum.com/southrad/conversion.html (5th July 2012).

★ ★ ★

Appendix E
WHO carcinogens

From list of 1020 known carcinogens [127]

IONISING RADIATION:

Alpha-particle internally deposited
Beta-particle, internally deposited
X- and gamma-radiation

OTHER CARCINOGENS:

Phenacetin
Benzene
Vinyl chloride
Trichloroethylene
1,3-Butadiene
Asbestos (all forms)
Plutonium
Arsenic and inorganic arsenic compounds
Beryllium and beryllium compounds
Cadmium and cadmium compounds
Coal-tar distillation
Phosphorus-32, as phosphate
Silica dust, crystalline, in the form of quartz or cristobalite
Chromium (VI) compounds
Coal-tar pitch

---
[127] http://monographs.iarc.fr/ENG/Classification/latest_classif.php

Shale oils
Alcoholic beverages
Aluminium production
Coal, indoor emissions from household combustion of
Coal gasification
Oestrogen therapy
Hepatitis B virus
Hepatitis C virus
Leather dust
Paint (exposure from occupation as a painter)
Processed meat (consumption)
Rubber manufacturing industry
Solar radiation
Tobacco smoke, second-hand
Tobacco smoking
Tobacco, smokeless
Ultraviolet radiation (UVA, UVB and UVC)
Ultraviolet-emitting tanning devices
Wood dust

★ ★ ★

Appendix F
Energy data

The data in this appendix come from several sources, and are for purposes of illustration only. They are intended to show orders of magnitude rather than exact amounts.

Physical Properties (at STP[128])

Sulphur dioxide:	SG 2.25 kg per cubic metre
Carbon dioxide:	SG 1.98 kg per cubic metre
Nitrogen dioxide:	SG 3.4 kg per cubic metre

Combustion Data:[129]

For 2,000 MW rated coal-fired power station	
Annual Coal consumption:	5,500,000 Tonnes
Annual Energy Produced:	10,825 GW-h
Mass of carbon dioxide produced:	10 million tonnes
Volume carbon dioxide produced:	5 billion cubic metres
Sulphur dioxide produced:	48,000 tonnes
Nitrous oxides (NOX) produced:	26,000 tonnes (as NO_2)
Solid Waste produced:	190,000 tonnes
One tonne of coal produces:	2 MW-h of electricity
One tonne of coal produces:	1.9 tonnes (100 cubic metres) of carbon dioxide
One kW-h of electricity requires:	0.5 kg of coal
One kW-h of electricity results in:	0.95 kg of carbon dioxide

---

[128]Standard Temperature and Pressure (0°C and one atmosphere)

[129]Derived from Macquarie Generation Annual Report http://www.mac-gen.com.au/Governance/MG990web.pdf 5 August 2008, 16-17

Appendix G
Known fatal incidents with ionising radiation since 1945

Year	Type	Incident	ARS fatalities	ARS survivors
1945	Criticality	Harry K. Daghlian[130]	1	0
1946	Criticality	Pajarito accident	1	2
1957	Alleged crime	Nikolay Khokhlov	0	1
1961	Reactor	Soviet submarine K-19	8	?
1962	Orphan source	Radiation accident in Mexico City	4	?
1968	Reactor	Soviet submarine K-27	9	40
1985	Reactor	Soviet submarine K-431	0	10
1985	Radiotherapy	Therac-25	3	3
1984	Orphan source	Radiation accident in Morocco	8	3
1986	Reactor	Chernobyl disaster	28	206
1987	Orphan source	Goiânia accident	4	?
1990	Radiotherapy	Radiotherapy accident in Zaragoza	11	?
1996	Radiotherapy	Radiotherapy accident in Costa Rica	7 to 20	46
2000	Orphan source	Samut Prakan radiation accident	3	7
2000	Radiotherapy	Instituto Oncologico Nacional	3 to 7	?
2003	Alleged crime	Yuri Shchekochikhin	1	0
2004	Alleged crime	Roman Tsepov	1	0

Year	Type	Incident	ARS fatalities	ARS survivors
2006	Alleged crime	Alexander Litvinenko poisoning	1	0
2010	Orphan source	Mayapuri radiological accident	3	0
			96 - 113	318

EXPLANATORY NOTES:

1. Criticality – incidents occurring in the experimental phases of nuclear energy
2. Alleged Crime – malicious use of radioactive materials – all in the former Soviet Union
3. Orphan Source – radioactive sources that have been lost or misplaced and fallen into other hands
4. Radiotherapy – accidental misuse of equipment used for radiotherapy
5. Reactor – equipment used for generation of electricity

---

[130]During an experiment on August 21, 1945, Daghlian was attempting to build a neutron reflector manually by stacking a set of tungsten carbide bricks in an incremental fashion around a plutonium core. The purpose of the neutron reflector was to reduce the mass required for the plutonium core to attain critical mass. He was moving the final brick over the assembly, but neutron counters alerted Daghlian to the fact that the addition of that brick would render the system supercritical. As he withdrew his hand, he inadvertently dropped the brick onto the centre of the assembly. Since the assembly was nearly in the critical state, the accidental addition of that brick caused the reaction to go immediately into the prompt critical region of neutronic behaviour. This resulted in a criticality accident.

★ ★ ★

Appendix H
Risk calculations based on LNT model

From the BEIR VII Report, the committee's preferred estimates of the lifetime attributable risk for all solid cancers and for leukaemia for men and women:[131]

Cancer Cases and Cancer Deaths (per 100,000 people)	Solid Cancers		Leukemia	
	Male	Female	Male	Female
Excess Cases from 0.1 gy (100 mSv)	800	1,300	100	70
Total Cases with no Exposure	45,500	36,900	830	590
Excess Deaths from 0.1 gy (100mSv)	410	610	70	50
Total Deaths with no Exposure	22,100	17,500	710	530

Combining solid cancers and leukaemia for men and women, we get a total population risk of:

Cancer cases and cancer deaths per 100,000 people	
Excess **cases** from 0.1Gy (100 mSv)	1,135
Total cases with no exposure	41,910
Excess **deaths** from 0.1Gy (100 mSv)	570
Total Deaths with no exposure	20,420

Note that these are approximations based on the inherent errors in estimating dose, dose rate and tracing the medical history of survivors.

---

[131] BEIR VII Report (Table ES-1), 15.

Appendix I
Nuclear hall of fame

A list of those who have developed our understanding of Nuclear Technology

Becquerel, Henri	Discovered radioactivity in uranium
Bethe, Hans	Pioneered the understanding of atomic structure
Bohr, Neils	Contributor to quantum mechanics and the model of the nucleus
Bragg, William and Lawrence	Father and son discoverers of X-Ray diffraction for modelling of crystals
Chadwick, James	Discovered the neutron
Compton, Arthur	Understanding of how X-Rays interact with matter
Curie, Madame Curie, Pierre	Original identification and studies of radiation
Dalton, John	Proposed the first model of the atom
Einstein, Albert	Developed theory of relativity and the interrelation of matter and energy
Fermi, Enrico	Developed the mathematical understanding of sub-atomic processes and developed the first chain reaction
Frisch, Otto	Pioneered understanding of the nuclear fission process
Heisenberg, Werner	Pioneer of understanding of quantum theory

Lawrence, Ernest	Pioneer of the cyclotron for acceleration of particles
Meitner, Lise	Pioneer of nuclear fission
Oliphant, Marcus	Australian physicist who saw the possibilities of nuclear energy
Oppenheimer, Robert	Physicist and administrator who oversaw the development of the first atomic bombs
Roentgen, Wilhelm	Discoverer of X-Rays
Rutherford. Ernest	New Zealand born physicist whose leadership inspired a generation of atomic research at the Cambridge laboratories
Seaborg, Glenn	Physicist responsible for identifying plutonium and other elements heavier than uranium
Strangelove, Dr	Just joking – mad scientist played by Peter Sellers and said to be a satire of Edward Teller
Szilard, Leo	Conducted the first chain reaction experiments
Teller, Edward	Participated in the first chain reaction experiments through to the first atomic bomb, and later developed the concept of the hydrogen bomb.

Appendix J
Glossary of terms

	Definition
Actinides	A group of elements form actinium (atomic number 89) to lawrencium (atomic number 103). Only uranium and thorium occur naturally in any useable quantity.
Activity	The number of atomic disintegrations occurring per second in a quantity of radioactive material (see Becquerel and Specific Activity).
Alpha particle	A positively charged particle comprising two protons and two neutrons (i.e. a helium nucleus) emitted by a radionuclide.
Atom	The smallest unique portion of an element. Cannot be broken up by chemical means. Comprises a nucleus of protons and neutrons plus orbital electrons.
Atomic number	The number of protons in the nucleus.
Atomic weapons	Weapons which use the energy released almost instantaneously when the nuclei of highly enriched uranium or plutonium undergo fission.
Atomic weight	The number of neutrons plus protons in the nucleus of an atom.
Background radiation	The amount of natural radiation in the environment. In Australia is just below 2 mSv.
Becquerel	A measurement of radioactivity in a radionuclide. One becquerel is a rate of one atom disintegrating every second. Named after Henri Becquerel who discovered radiation 100 years ago.

	Definition
Beta particle	An electron emitted by some radionuclides. The range of beta particles depends upon their energy and is up to one metre in air.
Cancer	Malignant tumour of potentially unlimited growth, capable of invading surrounding tissue or spreading (metastasising) to other parts of the body.
Centrifuge enrichment	A method for enriching Uranium in which the heavier U238 in the UF_6 gas concentrates on the walls of the centrifuge.
Chain reaction	Self sustaining reaction in which the neutrons released produce fission in other atoms
Control rods	Rods plates or tubes of a strong neutron absorber such as cadmium or boron that control the rate of reaction in a reactor.
Conversion	The manufacture of Uranium Hexafluoride from yellowcake before enrichment.
Core	Central region of a nuclear reactor containing the fuel and moderator
Cosmic rays	High energy ionising radiations from outer space.
Critical mass	A critical mass is the quantity of fissionable material just large enough and of the right shape to produce a sufficient number of neutrons to cause a self sustaining chain reaction of fissions within it.
Curie	The original measurement of radioactivity. Now replaced by the becquerel (see above)
Decay	The process of decreasing activity in a radionuclide.
Depleted uranium	Uranium 238, which comprises 99.7% of natural uranium. A weak emitter used as a shielding material, as well as for dirty bombs.

	Definition
Deuterium	Heavy Hydrogen - a non-radioactive isotope of hydrogen with one neutron in the nucleus.
Dirty bomb	A bomb which leaves behind radioactive debris
Dose	Amount of ionising radiation on matter.
Dose-Dose Rate Effectiveness Factor (DDREF)	The factor by which risk is reduced when the dose rate is low.
Electron	A negatively charged particle which orbits the nucleus of an atom
Element	A substance comprising atoms with the same number of protons. Each element has identical chemical properties, irrespective of its isotope.
Enriched uranium	Uranium in which the content of the isotope Uranium-235 has been increased from its natural state.
Fallout	The transfer to earth of radioactive particles present in the atmosphere because of nuclear weapons tests and other nuclear events.
Fast Breeder Reactor (FBR)	A fast neutron reactor that creates more fissile material than it consumes, using depleted uranium or thorium around the core.
Fast neutrons	Neutrons emitted from fission events, which travel quickly enough to sustain chain reactions.
Fertile material	Material not itself fissionable that can be converted to fissionable material. Typical fertile materials are U238 and Th232.
Fission	A process in which the nucleus of an atom splits into two or more nuclei with the release of energy and neutrons. These neutrons can cause fissions in the nuclei of nearby atoms. Materials that undergo this process (such as plutonium) are said to be 'fissionable.'

	Definition
Fuel rod	A tube containing fissionable material encased in a cladding.
Fusion	A process in which two or more light nuclei are formed into one heavier nucleus with the release of energy.
Gamma ray	A quantity of electro-magnetic energy without mass or charge emitted by a radionuclide.
Gray	Unit of absorbed dose.
Half life	The time taken for the activity of a radionuclide to halve its value by decay.
Heavy hydrogen	An isotope of hydrogen with an extra neutron. Also called deuterium.
Heavy water	Water made from heavy hydrogen.
Hydrogen bomb	Weapon in which the energy from an atom bomb is used to fuse the atoms of hydrogen isotopes, producing even greater amounts of energy.
Ion	Electrically charged atom or group of atoms.
Ionisation	The process by which a neutral atom or molecule loses or gains an electrical charge resulting in the production of an ion.
Ionising radiation	Radiation that produces ionisation in matter. Examples are alpha particles, beta particles, gamma rays, x-rays and neutrons.
Isotopes	Nuclides with the same number of protons but different numbers of neutrons.
Light Water Reactor (LWR)	Reactor cooled and usually moderated by normal water.
Molecule	Two or more atoms combined to make a more complex substance.
Mixed Oxide Fuel (MOX)	Reactor fuel comprising both plutonium and uranium oxides.

	Definition
Moderator	A substance which slows down neutrons and controls the rate of fission reactions. Typical moderators are normal and heavy water, graphite and beryllium.
Nuclear waste	Hazardous radioactive materials or materials that have been contaminated by radiation.
Neutron	An elementary particle with atomic mass but no charge.
Neutron bomb	A bomb with little explosion, which produces neutrons which are fatal to living things but relatively harmless to property.
Non-ionising	Radiation that does not produce ionisation in matter. Examples are most ultra-violet light, infrared radiation, microwaves and radio frequency radiation.
Non-stochastic effects	Effects whose SEVERITY is proportional to dose, such as fertility impairment, cataract induction, haematological changes. See also stochastic.
Nuclear reactor	A structure in which a fission chain reaction is sustained and controlled. Comprised of fuel, coolant, moderator, core and control devices enclosed in a concrete biological shield.
Nucleus	The core of an atom, occupying little of the volume but most of the mass and having a positive electrical charge.
Oxide fuel	Enriched or natural uranium in an oxide form used in most power reactors.
Photon	A very small particle of energy. Waves can be visualised as photons of energy.
Positron	Subatomic particle with the mass of an electron and a positive charge.
Proton	Subatomic particle with a single positive electric charge.

	Definition
Quantum mechanics	Mathematical descriptions of motion and interaction of subatomic particles.
Rad	Former unit of Radiation Absorbed Dose (1 Rad = 0.01 Gray).
Radiation	The process of the emission of energy in the form of waves or particles.
Radioactivity	The property of radionuclides of spontaneously emitting ionising radiation.
Radionuclide	An unstable nuclide that emits ionising radiation.
Rem	Former measure of absorbed dose of ionising radiation (**R**adiation **E**quivalent **M**an – 1 Sievert = 100 Rem).
Reprocessing	Chemical dissolution of spent fuel to separate unused uranium and plutonium from fission products.
Roentgen	Former unit of ionising force (no SI equivalent).
Sievert	The unit of radiation dose measurement. (1,000 Millisieverts = 1 Sievert).
Slow neutrons	Neutrons with low kinetic energy after passing through a moderator such as graphite or heavy water.
Specific activity	The number of disintegrations per unit of mass of a particular radioactive material.
Spent fuel	Nuclear fuel with high accumulations of fission products, inhibiting the chain reaction process.
Stochastic	Effects whose PROBABILITY of occurring (rather than severity) is proportional to dose, such as cancers and hereditary defects. Generally considered to have no threshold. See also non-stochastic.

	Definition
Tailings	Ground rock remaining after the desired ore (uranium) has been extracted prior to conversion and enrichment.
Tails	Depleted uranium (U238) remaining after the enrichment process.
Thorium	A naturally occurring radioactive element. Th232 is a fertile material that can be made into fissionable Th233.
Tritium	The radioactive isotope of hydrogen.
Uranium	A Radioactive material comprising fissionable U235 and U233 and fertile U234 and U238.
Uranium hexafluoride	UF6 – a compound of uranium and fluorine that is gaseous above 56^0C, a suitable form for enrichment.
X-ray	Electro-magnetic wave emitted from the electron layer of an atom.
Yellowcake	A mix of uranium compounds - the form in which mine product is sold.

Bibliography

This is not a piece of scientific research but an attempt to bring together well known facts in a way that laymen such as myself can understand them. I have made selective use of the internet and realise that much of what purports to be fact on the internet needs discretion. I hope my judgment has been adequate. I also realise that the internet can be an ephemeral source of information. Earlier internet citations are sometimes met with the dreaded error 404 and so any internet references include the date. If you get a 404, a Google search will help you find it somewhere else, or a similar reference.

Brockman John (ed). 2012 This *Will Make You Smarter*. London: Transworld Publishers

Broinowski, Richard. 2012 *Fallout from Fukushima*. Melbourne:Scribe.

Board on Radiation Effects Research, Division of Earth and Life Sciences. 2006. *National Research Council, Health Risks from Exposure to Low Levels of Ionising Radiation – BEIR VII Phase 2*. Washington: National Academy Press.

Bryson, Bill. 2003. *A Short History of Nearly Everything*. London: Doubleday.

Cawte, Alice. 1992. *Atomic Australia 1944-1990.* Kensington NSW: NSW University Press

Comby, Bruno. 2000. *Environmentalists for Nuclear Energy,* Paris: TNR Editions.

Fremlin J H. 1987 *Power Production – What are the Risks?* Oxford: OUP

Hall, Eric J. 1976. *Radiation in Life.* New York: Pergamon.

Ham, Paul. 2011. *Hiroshima Nagasaki.* Sydney: Harper Collins.

Hoyle, Fred and Hoyle, Geoffrey. 1980. *Commonsense in Nuclear Energy,* San Francisco: Freeman

Lowe, Ian. 2007. *Reaction Time Climate Change and the Nuclear Option, Quarterly Essay no 27.* Melbourne: Black Inc

Medvedev, Zhores A. 1990. *The Legacy of Chernobyl.* Oxford: Basil Blackwell

Parkinson, Alan. 2007 *Maralinga: Australia's Nuclear Waste Cover-up.* Sydney: ABC

Reynolds, Wayne. 2000. *Australia's Bid for the Atomic Bomb.* Melbourne: MUP

Rhodes, Richard. 1986. *The Making of the Atomic Bomb.* New York: Simon and Schuster.

Zoellner, Tom. 2010. Uranium *War, Energy and the Rock that Shaped the World.* London: Penguin.

★ ★ ★

Index

AAEC – see ANSTO
ABC Cancer cluster 104, 105
Absorbed dose 152, 153, 166, 168
Absorption of radiation 12, 31, 43, 65, 152
Acid Rain, xv, 58
Acute effects xi, 77–82, 91–96, 98, 122, 124, 126, 129, 143
Alpha particle 11–15, 22, 30, 39, 70, 142 153–155, 163, 166
Americium 12, 39, 67
Analogues 6, 42
ANSTO vi, xi, 134, 138, 139, 140
ANU xi, 135
Atomic forces 5
Atomic number 3, 6, 9, 10–14, 45, 51, 52, 59, 163
Atoms, 1-15, 19, 45, 164–166
Background radiation See Natural radiation
Becquerel, Henri 11, 15, 27, 161
Becquerel (measurements), 25–27, 65, 119, 150, 164
Beta particles 9
Biological Effects of Ionising Radiation (BEIR), xi, 70, 89, 97, 98, 99, 103, 113, 160, 170

British Nuclear Tests vi, 113, 117, 133, 135–137
Calcium (Ca), 4, 6, 42
Cancer, xiv, 6, 18, 19, 23, 41, 42, 77, 82, 84-112, 123, 126, 138, 143, 144, 160, 164, 168
Carbon dating 42
Carbon dioxide (CO_2) xv, 6, 58, 157
Carcinogens 42, 57, 84, 88, 89, 105, 144, 155
Chernobyl accident vxi 25, 30, 74, 78 -92, 87, 97, 100, 101, 115, 116, 120–129, 141, 143, 158, 171
Chronic effects 77, 81-87, 03, 96, 98, 110
Chronic Radiation Syndrome (CRS) 93
Clusters see ABC cancer cluster
Coal comparison 57, 58
Cobalt (Co), 15, 27, 41, 67
Cold war vi, 53, 117, 132
Cosmic rays 70-73, 83, 164
Coolidge Tube 20
Covalent bonds 7, 8, 153
Criticality 158, 159
Critical mass 48–50, 159, 164

CT Scan 30, 33, 74, 144

Cumulative effects 106, 109, 110

Curie, Madame 11, 25, 76, 161

Curies (measurements) 25–27, 65, 118

Decay 11–14, 23-29, 41, 43, 48, 59, 60, 70, 121, 131, 149, 164, 166

De Hevesy, George, 37, 38

Deterministic effects - see acute effects

Deuterium xi, 9, 10, 165, 166

Disintegration 25, 26, 28, 55, 70, 163, 168

Distance (as protection) 30–34

DNA (Deoxyribonucleic acid), vi, xi, 7, 83–86, 106, 111

Dose 28–42, 50, 71-114, 123, 126, 143

Dose rate 31–36, 73, 74, 80–90, 94, 96, 99, 102, 106–110, 160, 165

Dunning-Kruger effect , xvii

Earthquake 124, 125

Einstein, Albert 24, 51, 161

Elements – see periodic table of elements

Electromagnetic radiation (EMR) xi, 11, 15-21, 151

Electron 3, 7–15, 20, 22, 34, 36, 41, 71, 153, 163–165

Electron-volt (eV) 18, 22

Enrichment 10, 13, 31, 44–47, 67, 107, 135, 138, 140, 164, 169

Fission 62, 165

Frequency 15-18, 21–23, 167

Fukushima accident xvi, xviii, 25, 30, 82, 97, 115, 116, 124–128, 130, 143

Fusion 45, 47, 52,166

Gabon (Oklo) reactor 62, 117

Gamma rays 1, 11, 15, 17–24, 29-31

Geiger-Muller tube xi, 34, 35

Genetic effects 78, 82–85, 88, 89, 93, 94, 103, 104, 124

Half-life xii, 27–29, 39, 42, 43, 48,51, 62, 70, 84, 101, 117, 123, 144, 149, 166

Half Value Layer (HVL) xii, 31

Hard X-rays 18

Heavy Water 10

Helium 4, 11, 163

Hertz – see frequency

HIFAR xii, 56–59, 64, 134, 135

High Background Radiation Areas (HBRA) xii, 108, 109

Hiroshima 44, 49, 77, 89, 97, 103

Hormesis 110–114

Hunters Hill Smelter 45, 105, 131

Huygens Christiaan 1, 2, 21

Hydrogen (H) 2, 1–14, 45, 42, 53, 68, 118, 162, 165, 166, 169

Hydrogen Bomb 52, 53, 58, 162

Industrial applications xiv, 19, 23, 31, 33, 58–60, 74, 113, 138

Infra-red radiation 18, 135, 138, 167

Iodine (I) 14, 42, 117, 119, 123, 126

Iridium (Ir) 152, 67

International Commission for Radiation Protection (ICRP) xii, 102, 104, 110

Inverse Square law 32, 33

Isotopes viv, 9–11, 26–28, 39, 43–47, 59, 62, 69, 71, 102, 115, 166

Israel 66

Kerala (India) 73, 87, 109

Lead (Pb) xv, 3, 4, 10, 12–14, 31, 47, 57, 58, 60, 70, 149

Legal dose – see permissible dose

Light 1, 12, 15, 17, 18, 20–24

Linear no Threshold (LNT) risk model xii, 70, 90, 91, 96, 99, 106–108, 104, 143, 160

McMahon Act 132, 138

Manhattan Project 50, 52, 135

Mary Kathleen xii, 139

Medical applications xiv, xvii, 15, 19, 23, 27, 59, 74, 86, 87, 89, 92, 112, 113, 160

Mendeleyev, Dmitri 5

Methane 8

Microwaves 18, 20, 24, 167

Moderator 10, 56, 122, 184, 167, 168

Molecules ix, 2, 6–8, 12, 15, 18, 19, 83, 84, 166

Nagasaki 44, 49, 89, 97

Natural radiation, 69, 70, 75, 163

Newton, Sir Isaac 1, 2, 21, 22, 24

Nitrogen Oxides 58

Non Proliferation Treaty (NPT) xii, 65, 67, 68, 137

Nuclear accidents 115–130

Nuclear energy xv – xx, 44, 54, 61, 65, 100, 105, 113, 116, 124, 128, 138, 140, 159

Nuclear free zone xiii, xiv

Nuclear politics 131

Neutron 9–11, 48–60, 63, 71, 121, 153, 154

Nuclear weapons v, xii, 50–54, 65–68, 132, 135, 142

Nuclear waste xv – xviii, 59–64, 137, 143, 145

Nucleus 2–14, 161–167

Newton, Sir Isaac, 1, 2, 21–24

Oliphant, Sir Marcus 131, 135, 162

Oncology xiv, 23, 27, 41, 88

OPAL xii, 59, 127, 130, 139

Oxygen (O) 3 -10, 121

Non-nuclear disasters 127

Non-Proliferation Treaty (NPT) xii, 65–68, 137

Periodic Table of elements ix, 5, 6, 9, 13, 52, 148

Permissible dose xii, 87, 103, 128

Photons 18, 21–29, 31, 41, 99

Planck, Max 2, 21, 22, 24, 151

Plum pudding model 2, 174

Plutonium 49–61, 67, 107, 116–120, 135, 137, 155, 159, 162, 165, 166, 168

Potassium (K) 4, 65, 70, 72, 73

Protection 12–15, 25, 30, 34, 81, 99, 102, 107

Positron emission tomography (PET) scan 41, 139

Protons 2–15, 71, 153, 154, 163, 165, 166 Quantum theory 2, 21, 22, 161

Radio waves 18, 20

Radium 45, 65, 67, 70, 73, 76, 131, 149

Radon (Rn) 69–71, 87, 112, 119, 149

Ramsar Iran 73, 87, 108

Random effects – see stochastic effects

Roentgen, Wilhelm 11, 25, 152, 162, 168

Rutherford, Ernest 2, 162

Seaborg, Glenn 62, 162

Sellafield – see Windscale

Shielding 19, 31–34, 53, 56, 64, 67, 143, 164

Shoe-fitting fluoroscope 38

Sievert x, 25, 29, 35, 104, 152, 153, 154, 168

Smoke detector 39

Snowy Mountains Scheme vi, xii, 135

Sodium (Na) 4, 6

Soft X-rays 18

Somatic effects 78, 82, 85

South Australia 63, 64, 134, 140

Speed of light 12–17, 19, 51

Stochastic effects - see chronic effects

Strontium (Sr) 6, 10, 14, 42, 67

Sulphur Dioxide xv, 58, 157

Techa River 93, 107, 108

Thorium (Th) xv, 12 - 14, 57, 58, 73, 74, 149, 163, 165, 169

Three Mile Island 25, 82, 97, 116, 116–118, 129, 143

Toxicity 28, 60

Thermoluminescent Dosimeter (TLD) 35, 36

Thyroid cancer 42, 90, 117, 123, 126

Tritium 9, 19, 14, 73, 169

Tsunami xviii, 124, 125

UMPNER report xii, 140

Units of measurement ix, 25, 26, 29, 34, 35, 57, 135, 150, 152

Uranium (U)ix, xi, xii, xv, xvi, 3, 10, 12–14, 30, 32, 44–58, 62, 67, 73, 76,87, 195, 117, 131–145, 149, 161–171

Voluntary radiation xviii, 69, 74, 75

Wavelength 15 - 20

Whole Body dose 42, 103

Windscale accident 116, 117, 129

World Health Organisation (WHO) 84, 89, 144

World War II 45, 131, 132, 133

X-rays 11, 17–24, 29–31, 33, 35, 38, 39 – 43, 69, 70, 76, 86, 116, 142, 153, 154, 161, 162, 166

Yellowcake 47, 138, 139, 145, 164, 169

www.ingramcontent.com/pod-product-compliance
Lightning Source LLC
Chambersburg PA
CBHW071919290426
44110CB00013B/1419